Braided Organizations

Designing Augmented Human-Centric Processes to Enhance Performance and Innovation

Braided Organizations

Designing Augmented Human-Centric Processes to Enhance Performance and Innovation

Michel Zarka
Theano Advisors

Elena Kochanovskaya
Theano Advisors

William Pasmore
Columbia University

INFORMATION AGE PUBLISHING, INC.
Charlotte, NC • www.infoagepub.com

Library of Congress Cataloging-in-Publication Data

CIP record for this book is available from the Library of Congress
http://www.loc.gov

ISBNs: 978-1-64113-555-9 (Paperback)

978-1-64113-556-6 (Hardcover)

978-1-64113-557-3 (ebook)

Printed in the United States of America

CONTENTS

FOREWORD

Fabrice Brégier
Former President, Airbus Commercial Aircraft

During the last 10 years, Airbus—one of the world's largest airline manufacturers has been undergoing a major metamorphosis. Most recently the focus has been on its in-depth digital transformation which called for an introduction of radically different technologies to allow Airbus to instantly connect and quickly analyze the in-service data from all of the airlines via the Skywise digital platform. This new technology also enabled a full 3D continuity starting from the development of the new models and including the in-service cycle for the new generation of airplanes.

Transforming a global company such as Airbus was not a light adventure given the complexity of the organization, diversity of its multiple cultures, differences in core processes, and the large number of products it manufactures. In the process of this transformation, I have learned many things that, as Nietzsche said about building a house, "would have been very good to know before we began."

Among the key challenges were the large number of silos and layers, which had created significant obstacles to change, innovation, efficiency, and teamwork—all declared to be the core for the successful transformation of Airbus. Thus radical changes on multiple fronts were necessary for our transformation to materialize.

Braided Organizations: Designing Augmented Human-Centric Processes to Enhance Performance and Innovation, pp. vii–viii

We reduced the number of organizational layers, better integrated the different parts of the organization, defined shared processes, and aligned people and teams on common purposes and objectives—changing Airbus's culture at its roots towards more openness, connectedness, and transparency. Today I understand that many of the actions implemented were at the heart of an innovative approach to designing new types of organizations Michel Zarka, Elena Kochanovskaya, and Bill Pasmore called "the Braided Organization." With a much leaner organization in place, newly reconfigured processes, a digital platform enabling real-time exchanges of data and insights, we were able to remove barriers to collaboration and reengage people across Airbus much more strongly on shared objectives and a common purpose.

The hardest part was changing the mindsets and cultures, moving away from a pure task-based approach to fully-empowered, multifunctional ways of working, operating with full transparency and means of solving problems locally. In large organizations this mindset change must start at the top, with the senior team demonstrating first its ability to work together. The team at the top had to walk the talk—first! Looking back this was the pivotal factor for the successful ramp-up of the newly developed Airbus A350 aircraft.

While undergoing this profound transformation, Airbus was facing strong competitive pressures and a need to significantly enhance its efficiency performance. Leveraging the new ways of working with new technologies and digital platforms, Airbus was able to redefine the ways of working with its suppliers creating a much broader, integrated, and more efficient ecosystem connecting all of the players on the inside and the outside in a new collaborative plateau or braided organization and ecosystem.

Through this complex transformation I was deeply impressed by the potential which stems from purposefully connecting people within and outside the organizations—"braiding" hearts via common purposes and "braiding" hands and minds via open digital platforms. In this book you will find many lessons learned at companies engaged in similar innovative transformations.

Fabrice Brégier

Former President Airbus Commercial Aircraft

PREFACE

You may not be familiar with "braided organizations" as a way of describing organizational networks, but the chances are good that you are participating in one. If you log into Facebook or LinkedIn, you are part of a community that you and others have created, primarily to exchange information digitally. You belong voluntarily, participate when you are moved to do so, occasionally contribute something, and use selective judgment in deciding who you will and won't "friend" or invite to join your network. These same processes underlie the braids described in this book. The braids in this book, however, exist to serve business purposes, whether it be to spur innovation, coordinate activities, speed up project completion, or do important things that couldn't be done in other ways. These braids can be small and informal, or they can be huge and supported by sophisticated digital platforms. They can be temporary, formed around a project (this is where you are likely to find yourself a "braid-member") or more permanent, as in a network of suppliers serving a common customer.

To understand how they work and why they are gaining importance as a new way of working and organizing, let's return to your Facebook or Instagram page. You and your friends are a network, and you enjoy spending time learning what's going on with them without having to take the time to make a phone call, schedule a lunch, or actually visit with one another. It's convenient and under your control. There isn't really a serious purpose for sharing your photos; it's just nice to stay in touch.

Braided Organizations: Designing Augmented Human-Centric Processes to Enhance Performance and Innovation, pp. ix–xii

But what if one of your friends throws out a challenge to your shared network? Let's say he/she proposes that within the next 3 to 5 years, you work together to discover a way to triple your collective incomes.

You don't have to play; there is no requirement whatsoever that you do so. But if you do decide to play, your network has begun to form a braid—a small organization *with a purpose*. Things have become more serious, more *work-like*.

People who agree to take up the challenge start brainstorming ideas. Someone suggests starting a business. Someone else thinks that writing a bestselling book is the way to go. Others think about being more assertive when it comes to asking for a promotion at work. The energy in the braid builds as people express their interest in the ideas that have been offered. Your friend suggests that people should do some research on what would be required to pursue different options so that the group could have a better sense of what could actually work.

Some people start doing research and begin reaching out to others in their network who have done something like what is being proposed so that they can learn more. Other people drop out but then new friends become interested and opt in.

Things continue to progress and as the possible path forward becomes clearer, a brave soul offers to set things in motion. A small investment is required; the person puts money in a common "pot" and asks others to do the same. People contribute, surprising themselves by the amount that is accumulated over a very short span of time. Things are getting real!

The group discusses how to organize itself to carry out next steps and begins to think ahead to what would happen if the idea actually works. Some people step forward by indicating an interest in putting their energy into the project while others can't spare the time and are willing to play a supporting role.

As the idea progresses even further, it becomes evident that the group needs expertise that it doesn't have, perhaps in legal matters or raising additional capital. A quick search of the web reveals that a great deal of information is available for free, and that there are also organizations that would be more than happy to help for a fee. Incorporation papers are drawn up by an online legal firm that none of the members of the braid will ever meet. Another online gig-economy worker creates a website. Officers are named and the new venture is officially launched.

The first year is tough but full of learning. At each disappointment, people join into conversations on line about how the issue could be addressed. Broader networking brings additional insights as questions are thrown out to the wider universe and helpful strangers respond by sharing what they themselves had learned. The original goal is exceeded in just 4 years, with excitement high for what is to come.

As this example shows, there are many things that define a braid and make it successful. First, the braid needs a magnetizing purpose and a goal; it must transcend a few friends talking or sharing photos. Second, participation in the braid is largely voluntary; it's the energy produced by an attractive idea that draws people in and a mutual commitment that sustains the braid over time. However, in most organizational braids, the purpose may shift over time and the ways of accomplishing the purpose may not be completely known in advance. Coevolution of the braid occurs as interactions among its members take place. New ways of working are invented. That's why we say parts of the ecosystem become integrated or embedded in this new braided structure. Thus a braid is not separate or an add-on but is a part of an organization or the organization itself.

The braid needs a way for people to communicate, preferably in real-time. In this book, we are focused on braids that are supported by digital platforms (like Facebook, but sometimes far more complex). Braids need a way to expand and contract as expertise is required or work needs to get done. They must be able to reach people who no one in the starting group knows. There needs to be a core group of people who help bring about consensus and take action personally when required to do so. As we will see, in the corporate world, some people are assigned to operate braids; but even corporate braids wouldn't be successful if they didn't draw on the willingness of people to voluntarily do what it takes to keep things moving. That's why a system of shared governance must be applied to keep braids strong and vibrant.

Some things that *aren't* necessarily required are formal leaders, permanent members, salaries, colocation, defined roles, clear authority, quality control, detailed reporting, codified work processes, or performance reviews. A braid is a way of organizing effort but not an organizational structure in the classic sense. While reporting relationships may exist among members of braids, they don't always.

Clearly, braids are not formal organizations, but they are a way of organizing. They enable people to do things that formal organizations cannot do easily or at all. They enable access to expertise and data that may be needed to invent solutions or know what's going on. They build excitement and commitment through the meaningful engagement of people in pursuit of a common, meaningful goal. They are fluid and adaptable, making them perfect for knowledge-work that is critically important, nonroutine, and forward-looking.

At the same time, because they aren't formal organizations, many things can go wrong in a braid and there is no easy way to correct those things if they do. Because braids are often quite "loose" the wrong people may join, information that should be kept confidential may be made public, or members of the braid may do things that other members of the braid wish they hadn't. Key people may leave, causing the braid to dissolve. Or perhaps worse, the braid simply becomes another club where people like to interact with one another, but nothing gets done.

In this book, we will explore actual applications of braids in open innovation, entrepreneurship, supply chain management, project coordination, and corporate joint ventures. We will use cases that bring the work to life and provide a look inside the workings of braids. We will offer advice on how to start braids and what it takes to make them successful as well as what it means to be a leader in one. We will help you avoid some potential traps that are all too easy to fall into.

We are at the beginning of a revolution in the way we organize our efforts and work, made possible by digital platforms that didn't exist just a few years ago. New ways of working that utilize technology will become more widespread, for better or worse. There will be more virtual work and less face to face; decisions will be better informed by data but there will be so much information that it will be hard to decide what to do; we will become more dependent on people who don't work for us and whom we can't completely trust. We are already witnessing hacks, data breeches, loss of privacy and the gradual replacement of workers by intelligent machines. Along with these trends will be a growth in the number of people working in braid-like networks, be they full-time employees of an organization or gig economy workers.

CHAPTER 1

FLYING WITH THE SUN

The leg from Nagoya, Japan to Hawaii was estimated to last at least 120 hours—a total of 5 days and 5 nights. No pause, and just one pilot. On June 28, 2016 it was André Borschberg's turn to fly the plane—as part of a record-breaking mission to circumnavigate the world without fuel that he and his collaborator, a Swiss explorer—Bertrand Piccard had embarked on in March 2015. After 2 months of waiting for the perfect weather to cross the Pacific Ocean, André was finally given the green light to take-off. Japan to Hawaii was to be the longest leg of the entire journey and if any issues occurred, André could return to Japan within the first 7 hours after takeoff—but after that, given the prevailing winds, the Solar Impulse 2 would reach a point of no-return (see Figure 1.1).

Braided Organizations: Designing Augmented Human-Centric Processes to Enhance Performance and Innovation, pp. 1–21

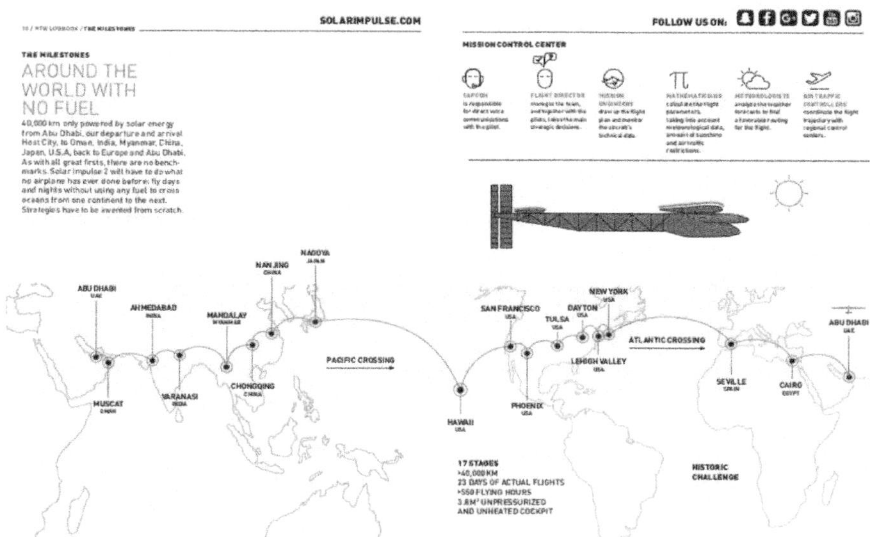

Source: © Solar Impulse | Revillard | Rezo.ch; used with permission of the Solar Impulse Foundation.

Figure 1.1. The Solar Impulse journey.

A few hours after takeoff, the autopilot monitoring the system indicated an issue—André could not be awakened automatically by the system if turbulence hits while he slept (the pilots could nap for a short period of time while in flight). But despite fixing the problem shortly after it was detected, the good weather over the Pacific and the perfect functioning of the plane, the engineering team insisted that Andre turn back. Had the plane returned to Nagoya, the grand adventure would probably have been delayed for months and even ended. On that day, the team whose success depended on flawless cohesion was in deep disagreement on how to proceed. The engineers having spent years designing and building the "unimaginable" plane wanted to bring their "baby" to safety and follow all the procedures meticulously. The other half of the team wanted to keep their dream alive. The tension was strong.

While in continuous dialogue with everyone on the team, André as the pilot in command decided to take the risk and keep going. In real-time, everyone had witnessed the debate, the thinking process and emotions through the continuous exchanges—exposed in real time what everyone thought and felt enabling a full commitment to the leap of faith decision finally made by Andre who announced to the team "Let's do this!" When that decision was finally made, there were no further disagreements—the core tensions had been resolved. The flow of conversations and exchanges

Figure 1.2. André Borschberg making the call to continue the trip on June 29, 2016.

enabled full commitment to the calculated leap of faith once the final decision by André, "let's do this!" was announced (see Figure 1.2).

On June 29, 2015, the Solar Impulse 2 successfully flew through its first night into the morning, when at sunrise its batteries started to recharge and use the sun to power its engines. Four days later, the plane finally touched down in Hawaii, breaking the world's record for the longest solar-powered flight by both time—117 hours 52 minutes and distance 7,212 kilometers (4,481 miles).

The overall mission was concluded successfully on July 26, 2016 with a landing in Abu Dhabi after competing 42,000 kilometers (26,000 miles) around the globe "fueled" only by the Sun. What is of interest,

Beyond the incredible feat itself, what was equally amazing is the way the Solar Impulse team had organized itself and carried out the complicated project work. Bertrand and André, the "Solar Brothers" as someone had called them, were the heart, gut, and mind of the mission. Although very different in the technical and professional backgrounds, together they became the inseparable *braid*—sum much greater than its parts. Bertrand a psychiatrist by training started out more attuned to the human side, while André the engineer was more comfortable with the technical challenges of the mission (see Figure 1.3).

Combining or braiding the two different knowledge systems and two different "predispositions"—the social and the technical, created a stronger combination of competencies necessary to lead a project of such colossal complexity, ingenuity, and innovativeness.

"Innovation does not come from inside one system" shares Bertrand, "It's not the people selling the candles who invented the lightbulb. If you want to innovate, be a pioneer ... change your way of thinking." This is exactly what the Solar Impulse team did, propagating these constant shifts of thinking, hacking of rules, while braiding the mindsets, knowledge, and experiences.

Source: © Solar Impulse | Revillard | Rezo.ch; used with permission of the Solar Impulse Foundation.

Figure 1.3. Bertrand Piccard and André Borschberg pose in front of the Solar Impulse.

During the initial design of the plane structure, when the first feasibility study was performed and shared with some large aircraft manufacturers, all said this type of plane could not be built to the specifications required. That is when Andre started to look for experts from other domains who could apply their knowledge and skills to building an "impossible" plane structure. And he found Decision SA, a shipbuilding company that designed and built the racing catamaran ALINGHI for the America's Cup.

Decision SA's knowledge and specialization in composite structure and carbon fiber was relevant to the structural requirements of the solar aircraft, especially its lightness. It took years to design and the structure but the final result was incredible—the revolutionary "clear energy" plane hosted 17,248 solar cells, a wingspan wider than the Boeing 747 Jumbo Jet (72 m), weight of an empty family car (3,500 pounds), and the four electric engines that together generated the power of a small motorbike (40 horsepower). After years of hard work, the impossible dream had morphed into reality (see Figure 1.4).

Source: © Solar Impulse | Revillard | Rezo.ch; used with permission of the Solar Impulse Foundation.

Figure 1.4. The Solar Impulse in flight "They didn't know it was impossible, so they did it." —Mark Twain.

While the original idea belonged to Bertand and André and they continued to lead the project, *there was no single organization behind it,* no organizational chart, no Human Resources or Finance departments. The project was funded by sponsoring companies, some of whom also lent expert knowledge and digital tools. Others inspired by the pioneering purpose of the project volunteered and simply showed up. Members of the extended Solar Impulse team worked virtually and interdependently from multiple locations around the world. The complex project which included inventing, assembling, and flying the plane on solar batteries was managed by people who had never worked together before and owed no allegiance to one another.

The accomplishment of the mission was extraordinary in many respects. Certainly, it required multiple breakthroughs in design and technology that some thought could not be done. It also required levels of motivation and commitment from all those involved that was able to withstand extreme uncertainty, risk taking, and high pressure of the mission. And finally, it required an improbable organization to form and function at the very highest levels of cohesion and effectiveness, without adhering to traditional principles about what an organization should be.

It was this latter aspect of the project that appealed to us, as it seemed to capture what we intended to convey in this book. Although we were not members of the project and the members of the project would not describe their organization in this way, we saw it as a **"braided organization"—*an intertwined network of contributors with different capabilities, not controlled by a formal hierarchy, who work together to invent ways to accomplish a common purpose.***

The Solar Impulse example, we believe, provides clues about the design of organizations for the future. We want organizations to be agile and innovative. We want organizations to fully tap the energy, creativity and abilities of the people engaged. We want organizations to set almost impossible missions for themselves and then accomplish them. We want people in organizations to work as if there are no boundaries, no turf wars, no barriers to accessing resources from the outside. We want organizations that learn, take in new information and then process it effectively in making timely, high quality decisions. We want leaders to know when to step in and when to step back and for people to assume informal leadership when they should. It seems that the members of the Solar Impulse team found ways to make these things happen. We stand in awe of both what the team achieved and how they achieved it.

In this book, we will explore different kinds of braided organizations or "braids" and provide examples that highlight how they are used to address organizational opportunities like improving the success of startups, alignment around core processes, and innovation. We will also discuss the challenges of working with braids, which can be daunting. There are implications for organization design and leadership which must be understood if braids are to be applied properly. There are also new capabilities to be developed around partnering, decision making, and collaboration.

We believe that the most important and differentiating attribute of organization design in the future will be the emphasis placed on networks of contributors —braids in other word. In order to be both more agile and efficient, the primary focus will shift from rigid, bounded, hierarchical structures to unbounded, fluid, interconnected collaborative networks. This paradigm shift will necessitate a redefinition of how we think about organizations, leadership and the process of organization design. Like the new composites that allowed the Solar Impulse to be built and flown, braids are a new kind of building material from which to construct organizations. But braided organizations are not for everyone.

WHAT MAKES BRAIDS DIFFERENT?

What can we learn from projects like Solar Impulse about the future of organization design? Our interpretation of some of the differences between these projects and a traditional organization are shown in Figure 1.5.

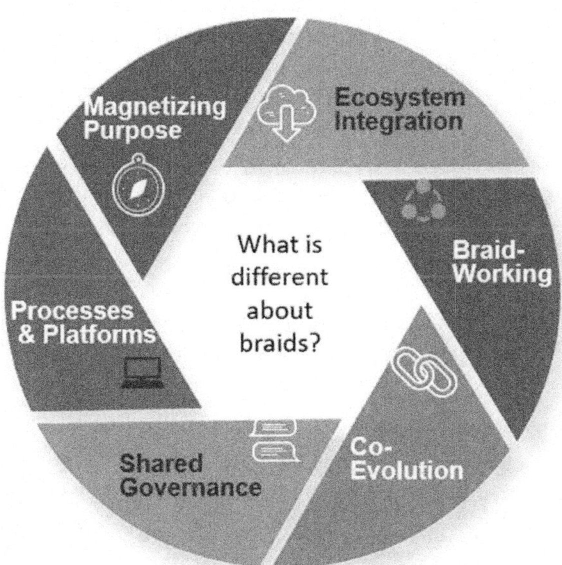

Figure 1.5. What is different about braids?

Magnetizing Purpose

All organizations have at least one core purpose and some have several. The thing about a braided organization that makes it different is that the purpose needs to be *magnetizing* to draw people toward a common goal who might not otherwise choose to be involved. Many of the most crucial actors in braids are temporary or voluntary braided organizations (we will see a large-scale example of this when we talk about the Red Hat and Electronic Arts examples later on). In the Solar Impulse example, it seemed to us that the purpose drew people in from the start.

In 2002, at the origins of the Solar Impulse there was no money, no team, and no technology. There was nothing but a dream, a crazy idea of achieving the first-ever flight around the world without a drop of fuel. That alone was an incredibly magnetizing purpose. Inside this same purpose was the objective to promote a message of sustainability and the limitless possibilities of clean energy solutions—“The future is clean,” the website stated. Anybody living on planet Earth who was concerned about the impact of the climate change could connect to its purpose. And many did.

Ecosystem Integration

Not all braided organizations tap resources in outside of the organization (what is referred to as the "ecosystem") but many do. Braids that transcend the boundaries of the focal organization and access expertise or resources from the organization's ecosystem are capable of greatly enhancing organizational capabilities or strategic options. For these braids to work optimally, the partners outside of the organization need to feel as if they are insiders. To allow this to happen, organizations need to be willing to share information, access to customers, influence in decision making and rewards. Moreover, the powerful effects of integrating parts of the ecosystem can be increased even more if the many parties in the ecosystem are connected directly to one another, rather than just to the host organization. We will see this in the Airbus example later, and it was certainly on full display in the Solar Impulse project (see Figure 1.6).

Figure 1.6. The Solar Impulse project contributors.

Just looking at the companies involved in the project provides some insights into the complexity of the project's ecosystem. From a company admired for its engineering expertise (ABB) to one best known for its beverages (Moët Hennessy) to an environmentally friendly city (Masdar), it is clear that members of the ecosystem brought different contributions and knowledge to the table. If they had remained as individual entities, each negotiating their role in the project with Bertrand and André, it is unlikely that the synergy among them needed to accomplish the dream would have developed. The representatives of these diverse organizations and groups seemed to create one team with a common identity, as evident from the shirts they wore; during the time they spent working on the project, they seemed to identify more with the Solar Impulse project team than their own companies (see Figure 1.7).

Source: © Solar Impulse | Revillard | Rezo.ch; used with permission of the Solar Impulse Foundation

Figure 1.7. Signs of the team's identity.

Bertrand worked meticulously promoting the project one company and partner at a time, sharing the vision, raising curiosity, and getting people exited to contribute. More than 60 different organizations joined forces with Solar Impulse. For many the mission of building a plane that could fly without fuel, thereby promoting the possibility of clean future, resonated well with their own corporate missions—sustainability, minimizing their carbon footprint, advancement of clean technology and innovation. These partner organizations contributed $170 million in financing but also shared their most invaluable resources—their expertise: people and technologies.

ABB, a global leader in industrial technologies, was one of the project's core engineering partners. The company deployed some of its highly experienced engineers to join the Solar Impulse team and help improve the ground operations control system and optimize the charging systems for the plane's batteries. Solvay—an international chemical and advanced materials company, sent researchers who were instrumental in helping Solar Impulse minimize the weight of the plane through its ultra-strong/ultra-light materials and increased the energy storage of the plane's batteries. Dassault Systemes, the world leader in 3D design software like CATIA and ENOVIA, provided access to their proprietary platform and software applications, used by the team for design simulations when building and validating the structure. Other companies, such as Nestle, were among the most unusual partners; nevertheless, their contribution was instrumental. Meals for pilots, the only "fuel" on board, were specially developed by the company's nutritionists to tolerate the physical pressures and changes in climate of the unpressurised cabin. Individually each partner brought in their core competencies, that when combined – seemingly braided into one cohesive team—collectively addressed the complexity of challenges faced by the Solar Impulse project.

"Begin with what you have, anything, and if you have nothing, work with people who will give you something "to have" and who will accept to be paid later," said Bertrand Piccard. This principle was one of the intangible building blocks of the Solar Impulse adventure. Having started with nothing, a few words on a PowerPoint deck, a vision, and the unstoppable drive of a few people with a common dream—turned a network of contributors.

The dedicated contributors and partners gave Solar Impulse more than "something to have." What they got in return was priceless both in terms of brand recognition, commercials spinoffs, and patents spreading across multiple fields (e.g., thermal isolation materials, solar energy encapsulation, lighter structures, lubricants, modeling and simulation processes among many others). Another important "byproduct" that emerged were the individual satisfaction and reward that contributors of the project experienced. Many reported a higher sense of motivation and pride that came from belonging to a partner-company that was willing to commit to the Solar Impulse purpose.

Braid Working

Working in a a network of contributors or braid is different than the typical well-defined job inside a company or the autonomous experience of being a totally independent gig-economy worker. Being a member of a braid means that you will need to be committed to collaboration; that the work will not be entirely known in advance; that your success and longevity in the role will depend on others' perceptions of the value of your contributions; and that you may experience quite a bit of tension as you work for the braid while representing your home organization's interest in the project.

The success of a project braid strongly depends on the competencies and contributions of its fundamental components: (1) the caliber of people involved, (2) the ways of working, and (3) interpersonal dynamics. In this regard, the Solar Impulse development team included more than 90 contributors, of which there were 30 engineers, 25 technicians, and 22 mission controllers. The final Solar Impulse consortium included the top talent from the engineering, mathematics, science, chemistry, physics, shipbuilding, insurance, banking, meteorology, and nutrition fields. It must have been challenging for these talented individuals to not only learn one another's technical languages, but to *listen*.

Each member held a dedicated and irreplaceable role on the team and was expected to bring forward their best knowledge and expertise. In parallel, there was a strong expectation that each expert listen to others (the "nonexperts" in their field) and build on each other's views and knowledge to improve the overall approach and find new solutions. Certainly, at the beginning, many must have struggled with the concept of coconstruction and this different way of working but soon enough (and through some dedicate interventions by André and Bertrand) they realized that there was no better option. Only by relying on each other's diverse expertise and different points of view could they discover solutions for each successive challenge.

Working together, they could push the boundaries of each other's rigid thinking. "Hacking the rules" was a requirement that was supported and encouraged. Patrick Corsi, the Head of the Solar Impulse Partnership at Solvay Brussels, outlined some of the implicit rules that were "hacked" by the Solar Impulse team (see Figure 1.8).

Successful projects depend on the ability of the project members to effectively manage the interpersonal dynamics of crucial conversations—conversations that are high stake, emotional and controversial. This in turn requires people to openly and honestly express their opinions, share feelings and articulate theories, even when they are controversial or unpopular (Patterson, Grenny, McMillan, & Switzler, 2002). Running as the "fil rouge" of the Solar Impulse project, the real-time conversations between team

IMPLICIT RULES ...	..."HACKED" BY THE SOLAR IMPULSE TEAM
A PLANE IS A HEAVY BODY, AS IT SHOULD CARRY ITS OWN ENERGY	When energy is available all around, the only issue is to be able to capture it. Plus store only the minimum vitally necessary.
PLANE STRUCTURE AND INTERIOR PROTECTION ARE TWO DISTINCT ISSUES	Biomimicry can help: some natural shells protect an organism living inside
AN ENERGY TANK COMES IN A 3D SHAPE	Solar cells are essentially two-dimensional devices, hence could "stick" on the plane's 3D envelope by means of special assembly
PLANE PROPULSION IS SINGLE SOURCE (KEROSENE OR OTHER, BUT CHOOSE)	Day flight and night flight reveal two disparate energy configurations under incident solar rays.
WHILE FLYING, IT IS ONLY POSSIBLE TO CONSUME ENERGY	Getting day solar energy can prevent elevation loss by storing potential energy for night
OXYGEN AVAILABILITY AND HIGH ELEVATION: TWO MUTUALLY EXCLUSIVE ISSUES	Molecular sieve nets enrich the little air available with O2 to allow normal breathing

Source: From "Way of the Solar Impulse" project article (Corsi & Michel, 2015).

Figure 1.8. Hacking the rules of aircraft design.

members never stopped. At each phase of the project, the 24/7 conversation stream was revealing the ideas, the rationale, and the emotions behind every opinion and position in real-time.

The project started as conversations focusing on a number of Solar Impulse challenges—"designing a plane that flies without fuel," "continuous flight—day and night," and "showcasing the possibility of clean energy." These discussions were fruitful and heated, as many different technical experts were invited to express their views. Later, the nontechnical contributors were added to the same conversations. The debates continued. These open discussions and exchanges between experts and nonexperts created an expansive range of possible propositions and solutions.

In this context, the informal leader's job was to sustain the "boiling" of ideas and solutions, expanding new concepts and filtering out the "non-viable" options. Certainly, some ideas had to be closed, while others remained open to allow the team explore new possibilities, morphing those into solid propositions. This ability to channel what to the outsider may look like "chaos," thereby keeping the team in flux and the flow of conversations in motion, was one of the most critical factors for the success of the entire Solar Impulse project.

Leadership Out of the Middle

The true value of a braid is in what the members bring to it collectively. In a traditional organization, there is a recipe; what is called a "business model" that specifies how money will be made or services provided. Strategic leaders create the model, and lower level leaders oversee its implementation. Employees in the most traditional organizations simply follow directions, but in empowered organizations are asked to suggest improvements in the plan or the way of executing it. Still, proposals are taken upstairs for approval; it is not a flat structure.

In the majority of braids, on the other hand, leaders need to step back because leaders of the braid need the help of members in formulating the plan and the processes for implementing it. There is a magnetizing purpose but not a strategy or known way of achieving the purpose. The reason for forming the braid is to gain the knowledge, experience, and resources that members of the braid bring. If these inputs are ignored, the value of forming a braid is questionable.

Allowing braid members to make decisions, influence strategies, and figure out how things should be done can be difficult for traditional, control-minded leaders. Control-minded leadership works when there's a known plan, proven methods, and superior knowledge on the part of the leader compared to subordinates. None of that is true in braids. Braids do learn, and processes do become more stable over time as solutions are developed and agreed upon. Still, the value of braids is in creating solutions and then evolving them in a world that is complex, unpredictable and ambiguous. This means that braids operate at peak effectiveness when there is a system of shared governance rather than individual leaders in the middle, giving orders, and directing traffic.

Certainly, over the course of the Solar Impulse project, there were moments when Bertand and André had to make decisions, like the one that Andre made to continue the flight over the Pacific. But even that decision was not made without the input of members of the braid. When debates took place and people with concerns were heard to their satisfaction, the leaders could move things forward by making the call. Leaders in traditional organizations would say that they often operate in the same way; yet the structures of traditional organizations make it clear who holds power and what the risk is of continuing to push one's position. Group dynamics experts have analyzed situations like the decision to launch the NASA space shuttle Challenger against the strong protests of the engineers who were in the best position to make the call. The dynamics of hierarchical structures can be difficult to influence and sometimes deadly.

Had engineers on the Solar Impulse project felt that their input was not being considered, their allegiance to the project would probably have faltered, leading to failure. In a braided organization, the most important collaboration is voluntary and needs to be maintained through leadership that is respectful and not overly-intrusive.

Lego-Like Structures

In a rapidly changing world, established organizations with rigidly defined formal structures have trouble getting out of their own way. People are invested in their positions and the power that goes with them. Ways of working are well defined and understood, even though they may no longer be appropriate. Investments have been made in capital, talent, systems and real estate that are hard to reverse. A huge advantage of braided organizations is the flexibility that they offer.

In this sense, the Solar Impulse project seemed to be a bit extreme. Since there was no structure to begin with, it was probably easier for individuals to adjust their roles and processes as the work required. Over time, contributors were divided into smaller teams each with a dedicated role. In building the plane there were the "configuration & structure," "energy and propulsion" and "workshop" teams. During the actual flight, there was a dedicated "flight mission" team that included engineers, air traffic controllers, meteorologists, mathematicians, a team responsible for tests, training and maintenance, and another one in charge of handling the plane on the ground ("the ground crew"). In parallel there was a "communications" team responsible for the multimedia and interactions with the press, partners and broader audiences on the ground. Finally, there was a project support team taking care of the day-to-day administrative responsibilities and requirements. These teams were not set out in advance; they evolved as the need for them became clear. Nor did these teams operate in silos; they could not if the project was to succeed. The project was made out of "Lego" pieces without there being a predetermined model that the pieces were designed to fit.

By the end of the project, many could claim credit for what was accomplished. Looking backward, the parties could explain the role they played and how they contributed. The engineers could no doubt recite the many breakthroughs that were accomplished, and members of the team could address the ways in which they resolved disagreements. When compared to a traditional organization, it seems that project members were not constrained by their "job description" but instead found ways to contribute when and where they could.

Lego-like structures, allowing real changes in how work gets done, the units that people find useful to create, and the choices that individuals make to work in different units over time are one of the characteristics of braids that makes them particularly well-suited to the world we live in, with its rapid rate of change.

Platforms and Processes

Because many braids stretch across geographical and temporal distances, advanced technology platforms that enable rich virtual interactions are often employed to facilitate the complex work of braided structures. Some braids rely on platforms that are already on the market (such as Slack, Microsoft Teams, or Google Hangout) while others, like the supply chain systems developed by Dassault, are designed and developed for very specific purposes. The purpose of a braid is to access and apply either knowledge or resources that would otherwise be cumbersome, slow, or almost impossible to bring into aligned, concerted action. The platform must allow braid members to communicate in real time so as to engage in mutual adjustment, make time-sensitive decisions, or undertake dialogues that have the power to shape the collective future.

In the Solar Impulse project, the Monaco Mission control center (MCC) was the "nerve center" of the project while the aircraft was in flight. A team of 30 engineers and specialists were continuously monitoring the key flight data via satellite links, analyzing meteorological information, calculating the best flight path, obtaining permissions for takeoff and landing, and finding solutions for any issues that arose (see Figure 1.9).

Source: © Solar Impulse | Revillard | Rezo.ch; used with permission of the Solar Impulse Foundation.

Figure 1.9. Mission Control Center, the guardian angels of Solar Impulse.

To keep the real-time audio and video link the plane was equipped with 10 cameras in the cockpit that allowed for the continuous exchange between the MCC and the pilots. The entire journey—its highs and lows were captured via a live-feed logbook available on the Solar Impulse website for everyone around the world to access.

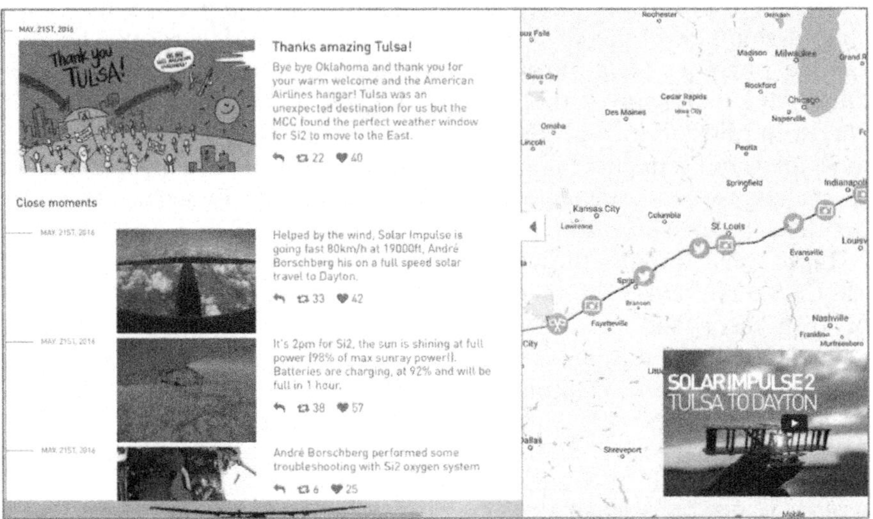

Source: © Solar Impulse | Revillard | Rezo.ch; used with permission of the Solar Impulse Foundation.

Figure 1.10. An example of localized social media that helped raise support for the mission.

The real-time connection was not limited to the Mission Control team. Bertand and André made sure to stay connected between themselves, to the partners and sponsors of the missions, as well as to the "ordinary" people following the Solar Impulse adventure every step of the way (Borschberg, 2017). Through frequent updates via online logbooks, blogs, and posts—the team managed to remain connected to the world of supporters and followers while in the air. The connection to the overall purpose of Sustainability and Clean Energy stayed live thanks to the regular interviews and communication directly from the cockpit. During the Paris agreement signature in April 2016, Bertrand Piccard spoke via video link with the U.N. Secretary General Ban Ki-Moon live from the cockpit during the signing of the Paris accord at the UN Headquarters in New York City. Piccard urged the delegates, "If an airplane like Solar Impulse can fly day and night without fuel, the world can be much cleaner" (Piccard, 2016). Without the right platforms to connect actors in the braid with one another and others in the ecosystem, critical work would not get done (see Figure 1.11).

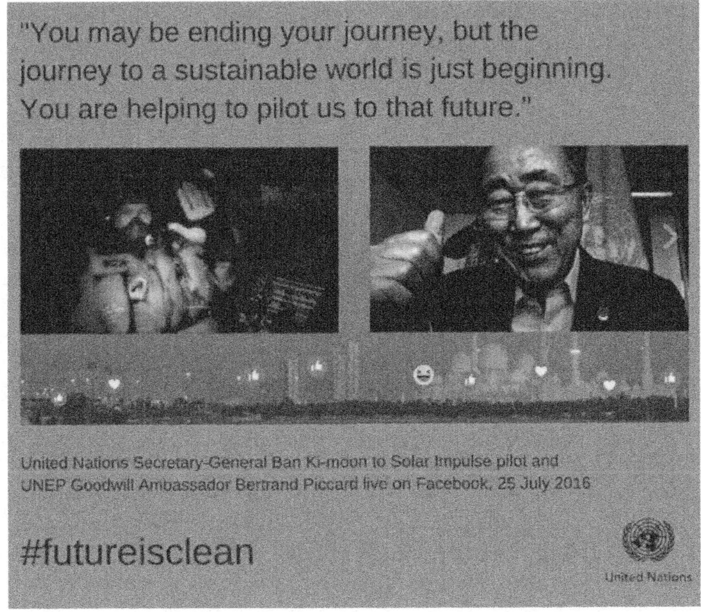

Figure 1.11. The UN Secretary-General recognizes the Solar Impulse mission to promote Solar Impulse website https://www.youtube.com/watch?v=r1EVfr0diZY

LESSONS FROM A PROJECT THAT SHOULD HAVE BEEN IMPOSSIBLE

What can we learn from the Solar Impulse project?

- That tasks that involve innovation may require access to resources outside an organization's boundaries
- That building commitment in a network composed of diverse contributors with multiple allegiances requires a magnetic purpose that overrides competing interests and centrifugal forces.
- That breakthroughs cannot be orchestrated through a project management system but instead rely on the spirited interactions among individuals with differing points of view, operating in a culture that embraces challenging the status quo and leaders get out of the middle to let smart people figure things out together.
- That the most important contributions needed for success may come from those who are not a part of the project at the beginning; and that the importance of contributions does not depend on someone's title or the company listed on their paycheck.

- That digital platforms enable real-time dialogues that produce synergistic thinking above and beyond that which would occur in a series of separate, sequential interactions.
- That projects or braids, while not full-fledged organizations, are a way of organizing.

THE FIVE CRITICAL CONTRIBUTIONS OF BRAIDS TO ORGANIZATIONAL EFFECTIVENESS

In addition to these insights taken from the Solar Impulse project, we believe the reason that we see more organizations experimenting with variations of braided design is that braids offer five key advantages over traditional fixed-hierarchical-bounded structures.

1. Access

Braided organizations are designed to cross boundaries easily, whether they are internal or external. As networks rather than hierarchical, fixed units with full-time members they can stretch to access expertise that is needed for the job at hand.

2. Coordination

Braids allow mutual adjustment without "going through channels" or other intermediaries. When braids are assisted by digital platforms, mutual adjustment can occur in real time, in some cases without human intervention. Because physical proximity is not a requirement in braided organizations, virtual work can occur across geographies and in an asynchronous manner that is not limited by regular working hours.

3. Agility

Braids are designed to be agile. Depending on the application, they can shift membership to bring in resources on a temporary basis that are not needed permanently. Braids can shift informal leadership at will to enable people with expertise to step forward when their knowledge is need and step back when it isn't. They can be temporary, meaning that a particular braid does not need to be considered a permanent feature of the organization's structure with the attendant costs and commitments. Based on what they learn, braids can change their direction, purpose or processes. Braids provide options that traditional structures cannot.

4. Knowledge Processing

Braids can improve decision making by bringing together individuals with specialized expertise. Working together in a collaborative fashion, sometimes assisted by augmented intelligence, braids can process information more effectively than traditional leadership teams. In traditional teams, leaders are expected to reach decisions on a wide range of matters that may be outside their expertise. Alternatively, leaders may turn to internal or external experts to provide guidance but then not fully understanding their recommendations, feel compelled to rubber stamp them. When designed properly, braids allow the best qualified people to have influence over decision making not as individuals but as a collective, leveraging the "Wisdom of crowds" dynamic described by James Surowiecki (2005).

5. Motivation

Braids allow people to contribute in ways that are important to them. The latest Gallup State of the Global Workforce report puts the proportion of employees worldwide who are truly engaged in their work at 15%. There are a number of reasons for this, including the fact that traditional top-down, highly bureaucratic organizations restrict the ability of individuals to influence decisions, constrain their freedom to contribute their expertise outside of narrowly defined job descriptions, put barriers in the way of them doing their best work, and provide jobs that are not inherently motivating (Hackman & Oldham, 1980).

Workers who join braids find almost the opposite work setting as that in traditional organizations. They are expected to influence decisions, are free to contribute in the ways they see fit and are asked to challenge processes that interfere with their success. The complex, highly collaborative, emergent work of braids fulfills the criteria for motivating work: task significance, variety, autonomy, exposure to a whole end to end task and feedback from peers and the work itself (see Figure 1.12).

We can only guess to what extent these five forces influenced the success of the Solar Impulse project, but we imagine they were figural. We will continue to explore these five critical contributions of braids as we discuss each of the examples of braids in action.

Five Critical Contributions of Braids

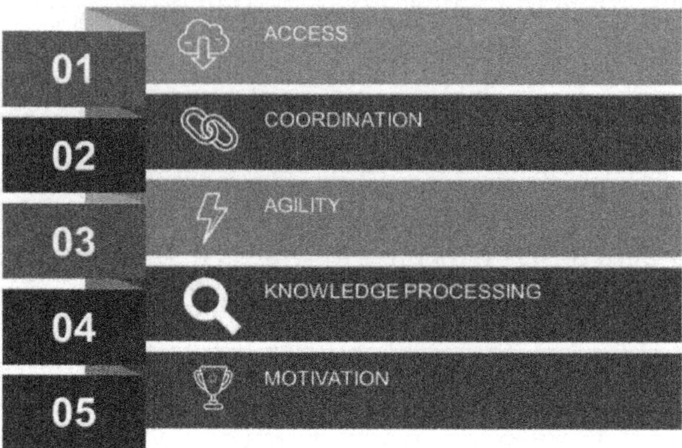

Figure 1.12. The five critical contributions of braids to organizational effectiveness.

THE ORGANIZATION OF THIS BOOK

This book tells the story of braided organizations: what braids are, how they are created, and how they can be leveraged. Braids can solve several of the key challenges we face in a complex and rapidly evolving world. Braids can help us span organizational boundaries effectively, whether they are internal or external. They can concentrate resources to work on tasks that we could not accomplish on our own. They can provide challenging developmental opportunities and motivating work for talented individuals. They can hasten innovation, unite us with our suppliers and customers, and allow informal-decentralized leaders to step up when leadership from above would be slow or inappropriate. At the same time, designing and maintaining braids can be a challenge. Their informality makes them agile, but also makes them more difficult to control in a traditional sense.

While not all organizations need braids, we predict that many more will employ them in the future to address opportunities for improvement that working in a braided fashion offers. Just as the captain of a boat needs to understand the types of ropes and lines that are available, and which is right for the task at hand, captains of industry and social change organizations need to understand how different types of braids work and where to apply them to their advantage.

In the chapters that follow, we answer the question "Why braids" by providing evidence that explains why leaders are turning to braided organizations as a solution to a wide variety of challenges that are not being met by traditional modes of organizing. Whether it is enhancing innovation, increasing the responsiveness of supply chains, or accelerating growth in a startup, we are learning that braids offer advantages that make them difficult to ignore. At the same time, creating braids goes against our conventional experience regarding organization design and for that reason, we should not underestimate the difficulties that accompany their adoption and use.

Next, we discuss the design of braid-based organizations, providing examples of how and where braids can replace more traditional lines and boxes. We also clarify how continuity can be maintained in structures that are designed to be constantly changing.

Then, we provide a range of examples of braids in operation across a variety of organizations. Although braids are a recent phenomenon, the progress has been impressive.

Finally, we discuss the challenges of implementing and leading braids, which are not insignificant. The appendix provides a tour of some digital backbones that are currently used to support braided organizations, although the technology in this arena is evolving rapidly and what is featured here may well be out of date by the time this book is in print.

CHAPTER 2

WHY BRAIDS?

The Institute for the Future is a think tank located in Palo Alto, California. Its specialty, as its name implies, is forecasting future trends. Its specialty is a 10-year forecast; 10 years is long enough to predict significant shifts in the world but short enough to still be reasonably accurate. Each year, the Institute updates its 10-year forecast. It has been doing this for 40 years. If you were to compare the forecasts done in the early years with the most recent ones, you would note a sharp contrast. The future has become more complex and less predictable, due to advances in technology and the effects of chaotic events that trigger unanticipated outcomes at the intersection of the global economy, the environment, politics, demographics, health, human migration, energy, innovation, and societal change. What this means, in brief, is that the world is becoming a less predictable and less deterministic place. Simple formulas like "Just work hard and you will get ahead," no longer hold. It also means that the design of your organization is probably out of date. Unless you are operating like an agile network that allows people to shift their attention from moment to moment and access resources from the ecosystem at will, you probably are not where you need to be.

Clearly, you would not be reading this book if you thought your organization was perfect—that it could do everything that it needed to do very well and more. In business, many senior leaders are recognizing that their organizations are not built to live in a world of increasingly

Braided Organizations: Designing Augmented Human-Centric Processes to Enhance Performance and Innovation, pp. 23–40

high uncertainty that requires greater innovation and rapid shifts in how resources are allocated. Most of what underlies the way we organize were conceived in the 18th and 19th centuries, and some features date back long before that.

Despite the world becoming more complex we continue to organize as we always have, with more concern for stability than for change. Although some are waking up to the fact that the way we organize may be the biggest barrier to long-term survival, many are still hoping that organizational structures conceived in a deterministic world will somehow withstand or overcome the forces of chaos. They are wrong.

Any significant innovation begins with a few early adopters who are willing to take risks that others are not. They learn from being out in front and as they learn, knowledge regarding the innovation becomes more widely recognized. Even with solid evidence that the innovation is succeeding, many remain skeptical and refuse to change, believing that the innovation cannot be trusted or does not apply to them. We see many of today's leaders hanging on to the past, trying to make outdated ways of working last a little longer. They cut costs, replace people who are failing, merge with others to gain economies of scale, delayer, streamline, decentralize, create centers of excellence, go lean, fire the CEO, simplify, go global, install new IT systems, adopt incentive plans, experiment with new business models, reorganize, and hire consultancies to advise them. While all these offer incremental improvements, they do not change the fundamental logic regarding how the organization operates or remove the constraints that are blocking a step-change in adaptability.

To unlock the organizational potential that is needed to adapt to a complex, uncertain and continuously changing world, two things are required. First, existing organizational structures have to give way to allow new ways of working that are more spontaneous and nondirected. Second, the boundaries of the organization need to be dissolved to allow people within and outside the organization to contribute to needed adaptations through their unfettered collaboration. These two requirements are supported by the use of digital backbones that allow people to work together in ways that were not possible when traditional modes of organizing were invented. New technologies are allowing us to work differently, and also permitting us to organize differently. We no longer need to depend on centralized control for coordination. In fact, centralized control is exactly what we *do not* need to adapt quickly to an accelerated pace of change. Organizations are going out of business at a record pace, in part because we cling to structures that give us a false sense of security in a world for which they were not intended. We still need to set a course and make decisions; we just have better tools for doing it that are more fit for purpose in the digital era. In the early days of steamships, vessels were fitted with both engines and sails; it was hard to trust the engines alone. We are sailing into the digital era with organizational charts that are the equivalent of outmoded sails, not yet convinced that we can function without our lines and boxes.

The demand for change is also coming from within. The foreshadowing of changes that will be brought about by Millennials and Generation Z are already visible. In just a few short years, Baby Boomers will give way to these younger generations, who are less motivated by money and security and more by "doing something meaningful," having an impact and being able to connect with others to continue to learn and grow professionally and personally. Raised in a world without boundaries, a world characterized by instant social connectivity and immediacy, our younger generations often feel stifled by the artificial boundaries imposed by silos, rules and job descriptions. We could ignore these shifts in preferences were it not for the fact that the skills younger generations bring are absolutely essential to the future. The hyper-competitive labor market for these talented young people is already causing the makeover of cities like San Francisco, Boston, Tel Aviv and Bangalore. Millennials and Gen Z'ers do not contemplate joining an organization for life. They know that they are likely to jump to new employers where the work is interesting, challenging and well-paid. Like many generations before them, they respect their elders but believe that they can and will do better at innovating, building successful organizations and saving the world. Their goal is not to take a long, slow climb to the top but instead to work "outside of the lines" on projects that are meaningful regardless of where they hang their hats. If traditional organizations do not accommodate them, they will take their energy and brainpower elsewhere. Google, Facebook, and Infosys are examples of firms that understand the demands of these young people. It is no surprise that they are ranked among the most desirable employers by younger generations. To compete, organizations that were built to make Baby Boomers feel safe and secure will need to change their employee value propositions.

Braids are a response to these pressures, a new form of organization that enables new ways of working. Braids are already in use in companies like Airbus, Renault-Nissan, Procter, & Gamble, Walmart, and Dassault Systemes, among others. They allow organizations to access information, knowledge, and skills in an on-demand fashion in service of innovation, improving collaboration, or enhancing operational efficiency. They represent the future of how more and more organizations and social movements will operate. They are a big deal. Using them in even a small segment of your organization can create significant advantages compared to current ways of working. Here's an infographic from Dassault that indicates why they are using braids to address organizational challenges (see Figure 2.1).

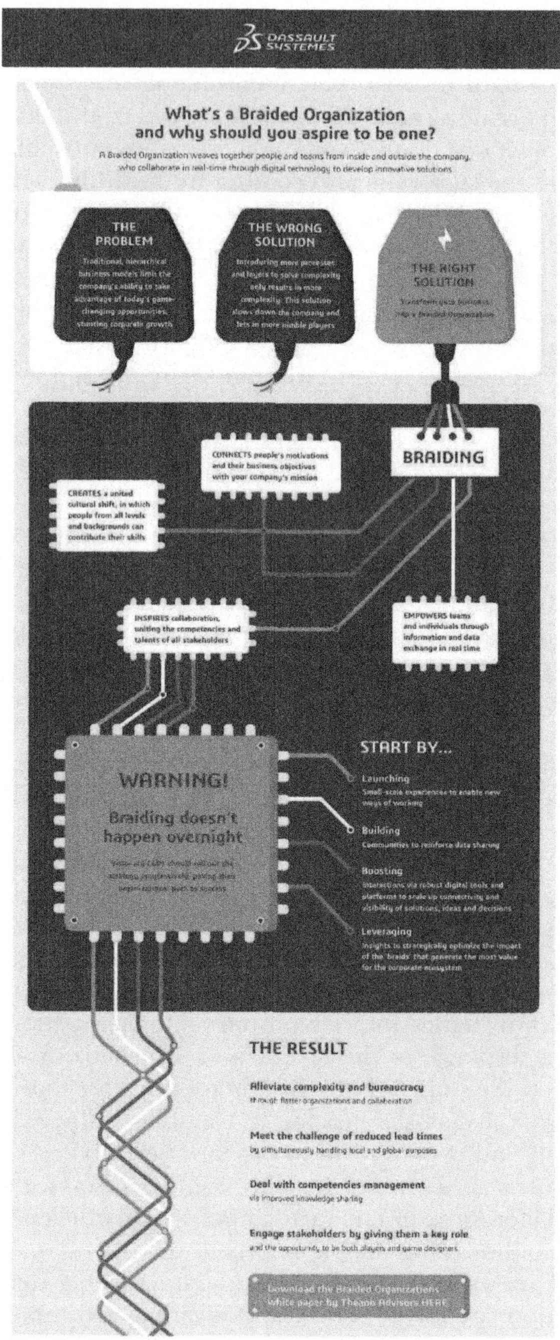

Figure 2.1. Dassault graphic showing the advantages of braided organizing.

A DEFINITION OF ORGANIZATIONAL BRAIDS

In the applications addressed in this book, a braid connects things that need to be more tightly connected. These things can be people, teams, units, suppliers, customers, investors, or experts. Modern digital technology platforms, built for the purpose of connecting such things, are enabling people to work in ways that were not possible just a few years ago. The underlying technology enables connections, but people still need to fuel and direct the energy braids can produce.

A braided organization is a network of contributors, created with a purpose in mind, often supported by a digital backbone that allows individuals separated by space and time to operate cohesively for a period of time that corresponds to the work the braid performs. The makeup of the braid can be fixed but more often is open, in order to allow new perspectives and previously unrecognized contributions to enter the conversation. Braids operate most effectively without a formal hierarchy that directs the contributions of members although processes and conventions often emerge to enable decisions to be made. The work of a braid is usually to share information, build upon ideas, coordinate efforts, solve problems, improve operational efficiency, achieve breakthroughs, spark new thinking or create new relationships. Braids can be commissioned by a purpose-holder or emerge spontaneously in response to a shared desire or goal.

To repeat the definition offered in the preceding chapter, ***braids are an intertwined network of contributors with different capabilities, not controlled by a formal hierarchy, who work together to invent ways to accomplish a common purpose.***

CHALLENGES THAT BRAIDS HELP TO ADDRESS

Braided organizations stimulate and sustain a steady, multidirectional flow of information, ideas, and knowledge among a wide variety of participants in the extended business ecosystem. This spurs the emergence of new connections between individuals, companies, agencies, and communities that often lead to new business partnerships and alliances with the capacity to accelerate growth through access to new technologies, go-to-market channels or customers.

Real-time access to business-critical insights is rapidly gaining ground as an important performance differentiator, whereas filtered information tends to keep people in the C-suite out of touch with reality and isolated from the frontline. Functioning as strategic and operational sensors, braids can better link the top of the corporation to the internal and external ecosystem, helping to surface issues and ideas. Serving as an independent alarm system, these structures can alert top management to operational deviations that may prove either detrimental or instrumental to performance.

Given their potential reach, braids enjoy a tremendous proximity advantage, making the scale more manageable. As a top executive from Dassault notes, "If you want to expand and support transformation at the scale on which it is happening in large organizations today, you can't have management and leaders in the middle. To let people interact and share, you have to get out of the way."

Braids create a new interconnected organization that is flatter, less bureaucratic and more able to leverage the innate human desire to connect and contribute. Braids provide a worthy and less expensive alternative to formal structures that make up the majority of organizations currently. Because individuals determine how best to contribute, their efforts are not constrained and limited by formal job descriptions or roles. Over time, as people make new connections and learn from collaboration with others, they find new ways to contribute that their former job descriptions could not have anticipated. Leaders in braided organizations do not need to "crack the whip"; they need to support the creation and effective operation of braids so that the full potential of a given opportunity can be exploited by using expertise and resources both inside and outside the organization. Restricting solutions to what is already known, what people inside can invent, on their own or what internal resources can support throttles back the opportunity to make breakthroughs that are truly game-changing.

Because the digital backbones of braids allow the sharing of knowledge at the speed of light, problems can be solved more rapidly, and lead times greatly reduced. Challenges encountered anywhere in the world can receive unrestricted attention from people with the expertise needed to provide solutions. Efforts to innovate can reach beyond known networks of contacts to harness the collective intelligence of a much broader and more diverse team of individuals. Thinking that is routine and hide-bound can be disrupted by voices bringing new ideas and perspectives. Problems that are too large, too expensive, or too complicated for a single organization to solve become more manageable through the contributions of many. Some of the challenges met by braids in today's world are listed in Table 2.1.

Increasing complexity, greater uncertainty. It is no secret that the world is getting more complex. Experts tell us that adapting to the rate and complexity of change we face requires that we "complexify" our thinking, invent responses, and implement change quickly enough to keep up or even get ahead (Bazigos, Gagnon, & Schaninger, 2016; Kahneman, 2011; Pasmore, 2015). Kahneman (2011), for example, warns us not to trust our instincts but instead to use data to make decisions on things like hiring people into important decisions or solving complex problems. Too often,

Table 2.1.
How Braids Address Some of Today's Challenges.

Today's Business Challenges	How Braids Can Help	Critical Contributions of Braids	Support and Evidence
INCREASING COMPLEXITY; FUTURE IS HARDER TO PREDICT	Braids provide access to a broader range of expertise combined with superior information processing	- Access - Knowledge processing	Johansen (2017); Pentland (2015); Surowiecki (2005)
FASTER SPEED OF CHANGE	Braids offer greater organizational malleability and more aligned execution, enabling faster change	- Agility - Coordination	Kotter (2014); Lawler & Worley (2006)
DISCONNECTED CUSTOMERS	Braids can include customers, enhancing their level of influence. This results in greater customer centricity, deeper customer insights and more responsiveness at the customer interface	- Access - Knowledge processing	Brown (2009); Martin, (2010)
FIXED LEADERSHIP	Braids allow leadership and leadership capabilities to evolve as the work evolves; braids enable ambidexterity	- Agility	Lawrence & Lorsch (1967); Tushman & O'Reilly (2002); Cross, Ernst & Pasmore (2013); Lawler & Worley (2006);
RESISTANCE TO CHANGE	Braids enable the creative self-destruction and rapid replacement of business models due to less reliance on full-time employment strategies and shared decision authority	- Access - Agility - Coordination - Motivation	Foster & Kaplan (2011); Pasmore (2015)
GLOBALIZATION	Braids enable greater global-local connectivity at multiple levels	- Coordination	Galbraith (2000)
SILOS	Braids span boundaries horizontally as well as vertically	- Access - Coordination	Ernst & Chrobot-Mason (2011)
DEPENDENCY ON A FEW CRITICAL PARTNERSHIPS, SOURCES OF SUPPLY OR FUNDING	Braids expand the number and diversity of potential partners without creating exponential complexity	- Access	Gattorna (2015); Pfeffer & Slancik, (1978).
INNOVATION	Braided organizations tap into the ecosystem to bring needed resources and expertise to innovation efforts	- Access - Knowledge processing	Whitehurst (2015); Chesbrough, Vanhaverbeke, & West, (2006); Huston & Sakkab, (2006)
UNHEALTHY CULTURES THAT STIFLE INNOVATION	The temporary nature of braids allows them to operate differently and outside of the traditional culture	- Agility - Motivation	Christensen, (1997); Kotter (2014); Bushe & Shani(1991); Zand (1974)

we "go with our gut" which is something we have learned to do based on our past experience, which may not be relevant to the situation at hand. The more important and complex the decision, the more critical it is that we intentionally "slow down" our thought processes to arrive at a better solution than our instinct alone would provide.

Braids allow better predictive capability with fewer inherent biases through enhanced access to internal and external knowledge, superior information processing, nonhierarchical decision making. If we think the way we have always thought, with the people we have always relied upon, we will get more of the same output rather than more diverse ideas from which we can fashion more complex solutions. Further, we need the people we count on to implement these complex solutions to understand them, be committed to them and move with speed rather than resistance. Braids are a great way to bring more complex thinking to the table and build understanding and commitment in real time. Digital platforms that power braids operate on the basis of objective data rather than opinions of what might be happening. They can help keep extremely complex and far-flung systems coordinated in ways that no amount of bureaucracy could.

Faster speed of change. Braids can be initiated when challenges arise or even beforehand, to help predict what challenges lie ahead. The membership of the braid can be configured to fit the solution required so that solutions are found more quickly and implemented more readily by braid members who are responsible for change.

The statement "Involvement leads to commitment" has been one of the most researched topics in organizational psychology and the data are not equivocal. If we want people to break down walls to get things done, we need to involve them in both the decision to proceed and the design of the methods to get there. When we do this with braids, using hackathons or agile sprints, people will work until they drop to find a workable solution as quickly as possible and then implement it. Contrast that level of energy to that of people leaving the typical management meeting and you can readily see why specially designed braids can be so effective at bringing about rapid change.

Disconnected customers who do not feel like "partners." We have come to view customers as part of a value chain, where their knowledge and insights need to be accessed directly and allowed to influence a multitude of decisions. Despite this recognition, the processes we use to engage customers are often inadequate to help us understand them more fully or include them in our conversations. Braids can be constructed in a way that makes customer voices more present and more salient in our day to day work and innovation.

The essence of design thinking (Brown, 2009) is to get close to customers through carefully planned observation, which leads to breakthroughs in product design that would not be possible otherwise. When customers are "brought into the room" rather than kept at arm's length, the conversations that transpire are capable of challenging misconceptions and changing fundamental beliefs. When this happens, new paradigms are likely to be discovered. Braids provide the vehicle to connect customers to strategists, designers, and problem solvers. Braids knock down the walls between an organization and the rest of the world.

Fixed leadership. Given the pace of change in general and advances in technology in particular, the ability to adapt in an agile manner to new challenges and opportunities has become critical for survival. Traditional organizations are designed for stability. One feature of stable organization design is creating fixed roles to which individuals are assigned indefinitely. In a changing world, fixed roles and assignments may impede the ability to react as structures, methods and capabilities required to do new kinds of work need to be put into place. Braids are more temporary than traditional structures, allowing talent and capabilities to match the work at hand rather than maintaining historical work arrangements. In traditional, hierarchical organizations, power is often used to defend oneself against unwanted change. In braided organizations, power is used to make certain that the right people are working in the right way with the right tools to accomplish the purpose of the braid.

Resistance to change. Inertia keeps us from making breakthroughs in the way we think and work. Often, it takes a voice from someone outside to help us see clearly what we already know: our current way of doing things will not last or will not take us to where we need to go. Braids help us to ask the question, "What if we blew up our current business model? What would we do instead?" and then provide alternatives for us to consider.

Globalization. Braids can be local or they can be global. They can even consist of "braids of braids" that help to integrate local expertise with global perspectives. Through integration, we can better understand local market needs and benefit from best practices or innovations that we might otherwise never see.

Silos. Even smaller organizations suffer from boundaries that arise between departments, levels, geographies, cultures, genders, functions, work shifts, or the external environment. Natural human processes increase our tendencies to pay more and more attention to the people who are closest and most like us, and less and less to others. Braids destroy boundaries and enable ideas to flow unimpeded.

Dependency on a few partnerships. Dependency on a few "locked-in" vendors can reduce the ability of organizations to control their costs and their destiny. Braids can help organizations become more "open" allowing potential vendors to bid on product or service supply, sometimes in an auction format. To take advantage of this potential, organizations need to have platforms that allow engaging and disengaging with partners quickly and easily, as well as monitoring the fulfillment of contracts, quality, and costs in real time.

Innovation. Organizations of all sizes struggle with innovation. One of the reasons is that both resources and expertise can be constrained by assumptions underlying the design of traditional organizations; namely, that the resources on hand are all there are available and that the innovation pipeline needs to be prioritized to fit budget and talent constraints. In braids, open innovation efforts draw upon resources in the ecosystem to expand the resources and talent available, increasing the speed and breadth of innovation.

Unhealthy cultures. We hear a lot about culture these days, as we should. "The way we do things here" makes us unique but also keeps us focused on the familiar, accepted, and agreed rather than the unfamiliar, not accepted, and novel. This was the message in Clayton Christensen's, *The Innovator's Dilemma* (1997). If we see ourselves as winners, the best of the best, we start to believe our own story. We stop being entrepreneurial and hungry and instead become overconfident and bloated. Braids help us listen to other voices, learn about new developments relevant to our world and question our fundamental beliefs.

For these reasons, braids offer advantages that are too significant to be ignored. Within organizations, in our communities, and across our world, there are opportunities that could be addressed more effectively by braids than the way we are currently working.

EVIDENCE THAT FEATURES OF BRAIDS MAKE A DIFFERENCE

Only a handful of organizations have adopted braids as we describe them here but many have experimented with "components" of braids, perhaps without realizing they were doing so. They simply saw a need to improve their effectiveness or to be more innovative and tried some things out to see if they might make a difference. In doing so, they started to create a body of evidence that gives us faith that the elements that make up a braided organization can truly make a difference in levels of organizational performance or innovation.

Access. In a 1,100-company study conducted by the Institute for Corporate Productivity (i4cp) in collaboration with Rob Cross of Babson University (i4cp, 2017), higher performing companies were 2.5 times more likely to be led by executives with strong personal networks that connected them to external stakeholders such as vendors, customers, and regulators.

The measure of performance was based on an index that included earnings, profitability, customer satisfaction, and market share.

Braids that connect companies more tightly with representatives of external stakeholder groups reap the same benefits and more, since the connections to the external world are not limited just to the executives themselves but to the larger set of members of the braid, some of whom reside outside of the organization's formal boundaries.

By creating its application programming interface, Apple enabled over 10 million designers to contribute well over a million apps that could be used on its products, producing over $100 billion in revenue for Apple. While this community is probably too large to qualify as a single, interconnected braid, the value of linking up with an external community of nonemployee experts could not be clearer.

James Surowiecki, in his popular book *The Wisdom of Crowds* (2005), provides many examples of how integrating the opinions of large numbers of people provides more accurate predictions of the future than listening to a few trusted experts. Braids can connect people together in ways that the voices of many can provide wisdom in making organizational decisions. Rather than relying on experts to map out the future in order to set strategy, Surowiecki's research would suggest that we would be better off asking as many people as we can to share their thinking.

Michael Arena's (2018) recent book, *Adaptive Space*, shares how General Motors uses carefully constructed social networks to link more innovative units with the parent corporation so that innovations that challenge the status quo are not rejected. Too often, large companies create innovation centers or incubators only to deny people in those centers access to power and resources. Braids are two directional; they allow large organizations to reach out for ideas but also allow ideas to find a home in established entities. With its "Connect and Develop" open innovation program, Procter & Gamble now expects half its new products to be developed by its network of over 70,000 external scientists the company accesses through its digital portal (Huston & Sakkab, 2006). Access to people and ideas fuels performance. The belief that a company is defined by its full-time employee base and the four walls of its buildings is as out of date as believing the world is flat or the sun orbits the earth.

Coordination

Returning to the study that Rob Cross did with i4cp, high performing companies are twice as likely to describe their cultures as highly collaborative and 3.5 times as likely to reward individuals, leaders, and teams for collaborating. It should be noted that such rewards are tied to business results achieved through collaboration in these organizations and not simply given out for collaboration in general. High performing companies are 1.5 times more likely to strongly encourage collaboration across internal boundaries and levels, and as we said earlier, 2.5 times as likely to encourage collaboration with external parties. High performing companies were also a whopping *8 times* more likely to have leaders who help others to develop strong networks—the DNA of braids. High performers were also 3 times more likely to encourage employees to report collaboration problems and to set specific performance goals related to collaboration.

In a study of 1,075 companies in 12 industries reported in the *Harvard Business Review*, James Wilson and Paul Daugherty (2018) found that firms that instituted practices that accentuated collaboration, such as reimagining business processes, embracing employee involvement, actively directing artificial intelligence strategies, responsibly collecting data and redesigning work to incorporate the use of artificial intelligence were 7 times more likely to show performance improvements when implementing artificial intelligence solutions.

Leonardi and Neeley (2017) observed employees in a financial services firm for 6 months. One group used an internal digital social platform to collaborate while the other group did not. The employees who used the tool became 31% more likely to find coworkers with relevant expertise to meet job goals. Those employees were also 88% more likely to know who to contact to find the right internal experts to consult. Those who did not use the platform showed no improvement in their network connectivity over the same period.

Braids allow a level of coordination of effort that could not be accomplished by traditional methods. People who design supply chains know this well since the obvious need for coordination led to the development of some of the earliest and now the most sophisticated platforms to support working in braids. Read John Gattorna's book *Dynamic Supply Chains* (2015) to catch a glimpse of how work in supply chains has evolved based on human centered networks supported by advanced technology—what we call braids. We are already into the fourth generation of supply chain management platforms that provide real-time insight into materials flow and predictive capabilities based on algorithms to better manage costs and fulfillment. The things we can do were simply not possible just a few years ago but we can do them now and because we can, Gattorna makes the case that we need to rethink the human organization surrounding supply chains as well.

Many leaders have been captivated by General Stanley McChrystal's book *Team of Teams* (McChrystal, Collins, Silverman, & Fussell, 2015) based on his insights from doing battle with the Taliban in Afghanistan. McChrystal et al. (2015) make the point that the traditional military structure used for command and control was no match for the nimble, unpredictable Taliban fighters even though our forces outnumbered them and were better equipped. Even by using a rather primitive digital backbone (basically a huge conference call) McChrystal was able to develop methods that allowed his forces to coordinate their actions much more quickly in response to Taliban raids.

Agility

Worley, Williams, Williams, and Lawler (2014) studied 424 companies in 22 industries to understand why some firms consistently outperformed others. Mediocre firms were described as "thrashers" because they went from one major transformation after another, only to fall back to periods of poor performance. The consistently high-performing firms, in contrast, did not wait for a crisis but instead adapted continuously.

Thrashers stepped back to redraw their organizational chart from time to time bit then "re-froze" into a stable pattern of organizing. While each change led to a temporary improvement, it did not take long for people to see that the new way of organizing had its flaws too. Agility was what led to high performance, not more frequent reorganizations. In the higher performing companies, agility was gained by tearing up the organization chart, not redrawing it. You cannot draw a braid as an organization chart because the focus and membership of a braid is changing constantly. The braid is adapting, without orders from the top. It is what McChrystal et al. (2015) discovered; you cannot fight an enemy that refuses to be predictable with an organization designed for predictability.

Knowledge Processing

We are in the early days of artificial intelligence (AI) and machine learning, but we already see tremendous potential in turning over knowledge processing work to machines that can do it infinitely faster and more accurately than humans. Brynjolfsson, Rock, and Syverson (2018) suggest that 60–70% of the work performed in call centers could be handled by AI in the future. "Siri"-like oral or written chat-bots have been demonstrated to be capable of answering a broad range of questions and "learning" as they receive feedback on the helpfulness of their answers. Brynjolfsson, Rock, and Syverson also point out that as machines begin to talk more to other machines through the cloud, learning in one machine (like an autonomous vehicle) can be passed instantly to *all* machines that could benefit. While this thought frightens many of us, it means that the speed of dissemination for certain innovations drops from months or years to seconds.

IBM's Watson is famous for making medical information more available to physicians and nurses as they diagnose patients. While physicians are "consulting" Watson rather than allowing Watson to make medical decisions, the cost savings and human benefits of avoiding misdiagnoses will compel further proliferation of the technology.

Even before AI becomes more ubiquitous, braids can help us perform superior knowledge-processing. There is a "secret science" that explains the effectiveness of braids when compared to other forms of organizing. In his groundbreaking book, *Social Physics* (2015), MIT professor Alex Pentland explains how social networks can make us smarter. While the "secret" is out, very few business people are aware of Pentland's research and the implications for how we work. The people who pioneered braids did so on instinct, not following a recipe from a book; but the fact that research exists to explain the advantages we have witnessed from working in braids takes the idea out of the realm of "fads" and squarely into the real, practical world. We will summarize just a few of Pentland's astonishing conclusions here.

Optimum idea flow. First, it should not be a surprise that seeking out advice from others can help us create more effective solutions. Pentland's (2015) research proves this but he adds a caution: too much influence by a few sources of information in a large network can lead to an "echo chamber" in which certain solutions become privileged over others, even at the expense of the outcomes we seek to achieve. The echo chamber effect is what caused the housing bubble to burst and nuclear proliferation during the cold war. Because everyone came to believe the same thing, no one could challenge the predominant wisdom until a disruption occurred. Idea flow slows when there are too few people in the network to stimulate new thinking but also when members of the network all begin to think in the same way. The most productive networks (braids) are those in which people are deeply connected, so that they can influence each other's ways of thinking, but diverse, so different perspectives can be adopted.

Most large companies are echo chambers. Leaders consciously or unconsciously tell people what to think. While being clear about the purpose of the organization is a good thing, as leaders begin to dictate *how* things should be done as well as *what* should be accomplished, middle managers and their reports stop thinking independently and adopt a company mindset. Braids have purposes, but their membership is composed of peers who have no particular allegiance to a given way of doing things. If the braid includes people outside of the organization who represent the viewpoints of customers, suppliers, marketers, technical experts, and others, the thinking in the braid will be much more diverse. Therefore, one underlying scientific explanation for the power of braids is that they produce a greater rate of idea flow, from which superior solutions can be harvested.

The power of social learning, for better or worse. Second, Pentland (2015) found that the quality of thinking done by people in networks is not strictly a matter of their IQ or creativity. A much larger influence on what people believe and eventually do is the result of exposure to those around them. People watch others without realizing that automatic social learning is occurring that shapes their conscious choices. Once again, in most organizations, people are surrounded by or interact with the same people on a regular basis. Behavior becomes "normalized"; we start acting and thinking like others so that we fit in. We accept authority unless there are powerful reasons to question it, and even then, we think long and hard before we take actions that might put us at risk. We start to live in a bubble of our own creation without realizing it. In our own research with groups, we found that the negative effects of social rigor mortis can be observed in as few as 6 weeks. The desire to fit in, to belong, is a powerful human need, even if it means we give up some measure of our ability to think for ourselves.

Braids encourage new ideas and different ways of looking at things. In fact, "fitting in" to a braid means that you bring something of value to the table: a novel idea or a new perspective that enables learning to advance. The currency of braids is not conformity, but idea flow. Braids are largely peer networks, which minimizes the risk associated with disagreeing with management or making a mistake. Ideas are comingled, built upon, enriched and applied, after which new learning becomes available to support further idea flow. Pentland (2015) paraphrases the Nobel prize-winning economist Daniel Kahneman, as follows, "We can consciously reason about which flow of ideas we want to swim in, but then exposure to those ideas will work to shape our habits and beliefs subconsciously." Organization designers have long been concerned about the right configurations of lines and boxes when they should have been paying attention to the stultifying effects of structural arrangements on people's ability to think.

Related to the above, modeling demonstrates that the best strategy for learning in a complex environment is to spend 90% of one's time in exploration and 10% of the time on individual experimentation and thinking things through. This is the exact opposite of what we often see; people who feel pressed for time go it alone, not calling on others for advice until things do not turn out as expected—or go horribly wrong. Braids keep people in conversations beyond the one that is taking place in their own head.

Taking turns. A surprising finding of Pentland's (2015) research on collective intelligence was that cohesion, motivation, and satisfaction with group membership paled in importance compared to taking turns—not allowing a person to dominate the conversation. At the extreme (and we know this is not true across the board) leaders who tell people what to think and what to do rather than taking the time to listen to what they have to say are destroying collective intelligence. Even if people are happy in a team, they cannot contribute their full potential unless they take their turn. Perhaps not so surprisingly, groups with women in them tend to outperform all-male groups. Women are more likely to be attentive to what others are saying, or to make room for people who have not spoken to get into the conversation.

The interaction in braids is often mediated by a digital platform. People do not talk over one another or shut others out of the conversation. People add their thoughts as they go, and others can see them. While people know some people in the braid better than others, social influence tends to be more equal. As people read contributions, they are likely to take in ideas they find useful or appealing, regardless of their source. Periods of exploration outside the braid followed by intense interaction within the braid produces a greater diversity of ideas, strong engagement, and the highest levels of productivity and creativity. The presence of "charismatic connectors," people who genuinely care about the issues and others, jet propels productive interaction within the braid.

In summary, Pentland (2015) notes that our survival depends on social learning; that we learn quickly and can influence one another. He observed the same network dynamics in teams and in cities. He warns us that the worst structures for learning are the organizations that most of us inhabit today. The more critical learning and adaptation is to your future, the more essential it is that you consider putting braids to work.

Motivation

We know that engaged workers contribute more than their unengaged counterparts. As it turns out, engagement in problem-solving, innovation, and coordination also builds productive, trustworthy relationships with others. Typically, people on opposite sides of a boundary—whether it be a boundary between departments, geographies or even the inside and outside of the organization—rarely communicate and if they do, their communication tends to be shorter and much less rich than communication within a team that is walled off from others. This leads to negative interactions, greater mistrust and a spiral of fewer, shorter communications causing relationships to decay. Research by Rob Cross and others shows that the number of direct interactions between people is a strong predictor of trust and the ability of one party to influence the other (Cross, Gray, Cunningham, Showers, & Thomas, 2010).

When problems arise between groups in organizations, the problem is often referred "up" the hierarchy for resolution. People at the top, who interact frequently, can usually work things out using collaboration to arrive at a solution. However, by stepping in and taking over, they have inadvertently reduced the direct communication from the people with the most need to collaborate. Trust declines and direct communication is interrupted, reinforcing the need to work through upward channels instead of working things out with one another where the work is getting done.

Braids allow direct communication and growing identification with others in the braid, even if members of the braid are complete strangers. It also allows members to more readily influence one another's thinking, which is the way that interdepartmental problems are solved, and creative teams make progress. Pentland's (2015) research shows that the highest levels of engagements in digital networks are found when the network grows in bursts of engagement rather than gradually and when people are invited to join by others they trust. As trust grows, so does the sense that success can be achieved. As success is experienced through interactions in the braid, motivation increases, especially when it's obvious to those involved that they could not have succeeded alone. Braids provide the support needed to create winning teams.

Access, coordination, superior knowledge processing, agility, and motivation are the five advantages that braids provide over traditional organizations in dealing with a complex, faster-changing world. Are you ready to give them a try? Before you do, remember what Dassault Systemes said—it is harder than you think and may not be the answer in all situations. The following is a quick test to see if experimenting with braids is right for your organization.

A TEST

Clearly, braided organizations have advantages over current ways of working in a number of situations. But does that mean that braids are the solution to everything? In our view, clearly not. Where there is no need to discover new knowledge, increase operational efficiency or enhance collaboration, the introduction of braids could disrupt a system that is operating perfectly well. Here are 10 questions to ask yourself about your situation that can help you decide whether to consider adding braids to the way you work (see Table 2.2).

Table 2.2.
Braids Questions

		✓
1	Would your work benefit from access to greater knowledge or insights from others?	
2	Would your work benefit from greater collaboration with others inside and outside your unit or organization?	
3	Would your work benefit from alternative ways of working or novel solutions to problems/opportunities?	
4	Would your work benefit from increased operational efficiency?	
5	Is your work likely to be disrupted by faster, smarter, cheaper or more innovative competitors?	
6	Are you interested in making your organization more innovative or more efficient?	
7	Are you willing to experiment with novel solutions or different ways of working?	
8	Are you willing to be influenced by people with different expertise or points of view?	
9	Are you willing to share your challenges and opportunities with others as well as the intellectual property they might help to create?	
10	Are you willing to invest time and resources in learning how to make a braided organization work?	

Should You Braid? A Quick Test

Instructions: Check the boxes that apply to your situation. If you checked 0–3 boxes, you probably should continue what you are doing without using braids. If you checked 4–6 boxes, you should give some careful consideration to how braided organizations might help. If you score 7–10, what are you waiting for? Start experimenting with braids immediately!

CHAPTER 3

BRAIDED ORGANIZATION DESIGN

We live in an era of digital Darwinism," writes Brian Solis (2014), an award-winning futurist and digital analyst. "As customer expectations evolve and move toward personalized experiences and beyond transactions, companies in every industry must focus digital transformation on not only digital, but also people, purpose, and relevance." The ability to adapt has never been so critical; and yet, the formal designs of many organizations constrain progress. We think about organization design as lines and boxes. Leaders who wish their organizations were more agile may daydream about doing away with the lines and boxes, but what then? Instead of neatly ordered cubicles, should we create open-space floor plans, install foosball tables, and throw away the organization chart? What happens then? We vacillate between traditional structures and no structure at all because we aren't aware of other options that make sense. We still need to be able to create a vision, set goals, design processes and get people to work in an aligned fashion. How does that all happen spontaneously, and without direction from above? Is there something in between bureaucracy and chaos? Actually, there is; braided organization design.

Braided Organizations: Designing Augmented Human-Centric Processes to Enhance Performance and Innovation, pp. 41–70

FORMAL COMPONENTS OF BRAIDED ORGANIZATION DESIGN

The frustrations that leaders feel with traditional bureaucratic organizational structures are driving them to consider different ways of organizing. Traditional structures are slow to change, make it exceedingly difficult for units to work interdependently, are not responsive enough to customers, are too inwardly-focused and fail to provide motivating work to a majority of employees. There seems to be a growing consensus emerging that organizations of the future will be flatter, more agile, team-based, built around networks that connect suppliers to customers, and rely more on gig-economy workers (Lawler & Worley, 2006; Page, Rahnema, Murphy, & McDowell, 2016).

A number of forces have combined to produce this trend in our thinking. The rapid growth of platform-based organizations like Google and Facebook, who ushered in an era of younger workforces and less restrictive roles, made it seem that innovation, talent and organization design were somehow connected. At the same time, the popularity of design thinking, championed by IDEO and other firms, made it appear that a fun, team-based culture was the key to creativity. Then, open innovators like Procter & Gamble and Red Hat demonstrated the wisdom of seeking help from the ecosystem in generating ideas or solutions to difficult challenges. A few well-publicized outliers, including Zappos which employed a structure called a "holacracy" (Bernstein, Bunch, Canner, & Lee (2016) and W.L. Gore which de-emphasized formal roles and allowed employees to vote for their CEO (Manz, Shipper, & Stewart, 2009) stood as proof that there were alternatives to traditional organizing that not only worked but produced compelling results. Enterprise resource planning (ERP) systems enabled tight coordination among players in value chains that didn't require control from above. Traditional organizations had long employed "task forces" or project teams to operate outside of the organization's usual structure and processes to enable more rapid progress in addressing opportunities or crises (Zand, 1974; Bushe & Shani, 1991). Some forms created incubators or Silicon Valley outposts to defy tradition and hasten innovation. In our view, all of these forces have combined to lead us to an interest in how to organize differently. The consistent answer seems to lie in utilizing technology to support less hierarchical, more agile, self-controlling, and more motivating ways of working. Braided organization design is a reflection of this new direction.

Figure 3.1 is one way to depict the formal aspects of braided organization design. It serves as a kind of Rosetta stone, allowing the language of braids to be interpreted as a series of design choices. Once the language is understood, it is a relatively straightforward matter to begin using braids to address organizational challenges and opportunities that are not easily handled through traditional organizational designs.

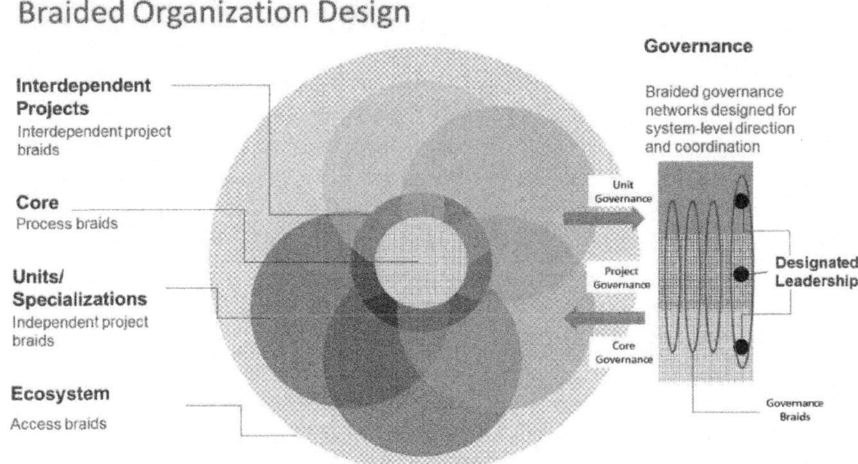

Figure 3.1. Components of braided organization designs.

Core Process Braids

In their thinking about ambidextrous organizations, Tushman and O'Reilly (2002) call for ambidextrous organization designs that allow for a stable, rigid core of operations and an innovative, less constrained part of the structure that is designed to support experimentation and change. The organizations profiled in this book vary in how rigid their cores are; from the Solar Impulse project that had no need for a rigid core to Airbus, for whom a rigid core is absolutely essential to the repeatable, safe, cost efficient production of aircraft.

Even in the core of organizations like Airbus or Dassault Systèmes, braids can enable the collaborative work that is required to coordinated activities of thousands of people, representing different functions, geographies, organizations and areas of expertise. The breakthrough thinking introduced by process reengineers like Davenport (1993) and Hammer and Champy (1993) was that work should be thought of horizontally versus vertically, meaning that what went on between units and departments was more important than what went on within them. Lean manufacturing and quality efforts like Six Sigma built upon and reinforced this philosophy. Braided organization design takes this one step further. Reengineering efforts, lean and Six Sigma are intended as overlays on the disjointed, siloed, hierarchical structure that are so characteristic of traditional production operations. Braids structures replace this traditional structure with horizontal teams that coordinate with one another to ensure that production processes, quality, safety, and supply are flowing smoothly and effectively. Control is provided both by technology (the shared digital backbone that updates information in real time and allows adjustments in work to remain coordinated) and the knowledge of the people closest to the work, who are communicating with one another using platforms and governance structures designed to align information, expertise, and decision-making authority. In the case of Airbus, as we shall see, the core braids extend beyond the walls of Airbus, since suppliers are essential to the timely, cost-effective, successful completion of aircraft construction.

Independent Unit Braids

Even in braided organizations there are centers of excellence, communities of expertise, geographical or product-based business units, and other groups or teams that share a common identity. In a traditional organization, these entities would be shown as stand-alone boxes on an organization chart. In Figure 3.1 they are depicted as circles surrounding the core, supporting it but not entirely captured within it. They also face outward, toward the organization's ecosystem, drawing in expertise and coordinating activities with suppliers and customers.

At times, the independent units act independently; they do the work that they are uniquely qualified to do, such as human resource administering benefits or finance auditing budgets. The focus on independent unit braids vary by the specific strategies and circumstances of the organization in question. The units are not permanent but rather can change in number or nature as the need for new specialized work becomes apparent.

At other times, the independent units join into collaborative projects with other units, forming *interdependent projects* that require cross-unit braids. Examples of these projects include introducing new products, enhancing value chain connections, or opening up a new territory. These projects require extensive collaboration in which each unit must bring its specialized expertise to bear on the challenge at hand. The interdependent project braid is composed of the individuals who represent the expertise of their units and who will work together to meld that expertise into a workable solution. That solution will not be what each unit would have done if working alone but rather a solution that optimizes the overall outcomes even if it suboptimizes what the units could have contributed. For example, in designing a platform for improving the customer interface, many "bells and whistles" that could be built into the platform may be left out because they overcomplicate the system, making it difficult to learn and use. The value of the interdependent project braid is fully demonstrated when the expertise of its individual members is balanced by the diversity of perspectives and wisdom of the whole.

Ecosystem Access Braids

Ecosystem access braids are those that extend beyond the boundaries of the host organization. They occur when suppliers, customers, contractors or open-innovation collaborators are engaged in projects or sustained relationships with the host organization and connected by a shared platform. The key is that these braids are relationship-based, not simply an arms-length or one-off transaction. They require collaboration across the host organization's boundary, engendering the kind of collaborative work that one usually thinks of as only occurring within the organization itself.

Ecosystem access braids are becoming increasingly important for the reasons noted in the chapter "Why Braids"; they provide access to expertise, enable joint adaptation to change, and ease the process of mutual adjustment in service of work toward shared goals. The Solar Impulse project was almost entirely an ecosystem braid, which is what made it such a remarkable example.

Governance Braids

Governance braids largely replace the lines and boxes that we see in traditional organizational charts. The term "governance" brings to mind images of regulatory enforcement or boardroom bylaws. Here, we use the term simply to indicate how decisions are made. In formal organizations, decisions are made by those occupying leadership roles in the hierarchy. Decisions can be delegated, of course, but what decisions are delegated, and the degree of review required is determined by formal leaders who hold positions of power.

In braids, decisions are made by many people, some of whom may have titles that convey authority and others who do not. In some cases, who makes decisions can change rapidly as the expertise needed to make the best decision in a specific instance shifts from person to person or group to group. At first, this system of governance probably sounds messy and slow. In reality, it is anything but.

The principles behind governance in braids are captured in Table 3.1. These principles are based on research that investigated processes for optimizing decision making under conditions of uncertainty (Pava, 1983; Purser, Pasmore, & Tenkasi, 1992). It is these principles that make braid governance a superior approach to decision making when facing situations that are rapidly changing and where answers can't be derived from past experience alone.

Table 3.1.
Principles of Braid Governance

PRINCIPLE	EXPLANATION
Knowledge not titles	People with relevant expertise, first-hand experience and closest to the action are included in the process; conversely, people with no direct experience or relevant knowledge are not automatically included simply because of their title
Include the doers	Include the people expected to carry out the decision in making it. Decisions that affect more than one unit require representatives from the units to collaborate in decision making
Respect the process	Processes that guide how people interact allow people with contributions to be heard and their inputs given weight in decisions. Failure to follow processes that are designed to enhance knowledge processing through conversations result in subpar decisions
Access wisdom	Invoke expertise, even if outside the organization, rather than deciding based only on the knowledge at hand
Make the right decision the first time	Speed is sometimes necessary but over-utilized as an excuse for not listening carefully to opposing opinions or acknowledging that a decision is based on a guess. Once decisions are made, the time and cost of reversing them can be prohibitive, compounding initial bad decisions with more in turn
Document to verify	Taking the time to document decisions and actions before adjourning prevents people from leaving governance meetings with different understandings of what was decided

Governance in a braided organization can take several forms. To maintain an overall strategic direction until it is time to change it, a "leadership braid" can be created. The leadership braid can be composed of representatives of other braids and stand for terms of office that are longer than those of other braid leaders. These individuals are referred to as "designated leadership" in Figure 3.1. Designated leaders in braided organizations do not have absolute power except in emergencies, can rotate back into other roles in the organization after serving in the leadership braid, and are expected to represent the entire organization and its ecosystem rather than a single unit. This makes the leadership braid different than the typical executive team.

Representatives of units involved in collaborative projects can come together to form *project governance braids*, and representatives of units can be engaged in decisions with the leadership braid. These individuals should not be designated as "permanent representatives." Rather, the people involved in governance decisions, following the principles of governance outlined in Table 3.1, should change depending upon the nature of the decisions being made.

This approach to governance provides the agility that organizations in a fast-changing world require. Traditional structures allow decisions to be made quickly but sometimes incorrectly, separate decision makers from doers, and result in frequent failures to execute strategies.

INFORMAL COMPONENTS OF BRAIDED ORGANIZATION DESIGN

Just as important as the formal components of braided organizational design are the informal components, having to do with talent and culture. In order to fully leverage the power of braids, behavior can't be left to chance. Instead, clear expectations that shape the culture to work as intended need to be spelled out. Table 3.2 outlines some of the design components for culture and talent in braided organizations in contrast to more traditional ones.

It is easy to see the components described in Table 3.2 in the working of the Solar Impulse project organization. With very little formality and few constraints, the team was able to leverage its talents to achieve remarkable performance. But what if the Solar Impulse team became a "real" organization? How would it preserve its culture over time? This is exactly the challenge that startups face as they grow; while going from informal, relationship-based, unstructured teams to giant enterprises, the risk of losing the founding culture is great. Once the culture is lost, it is hard to get it back again. This is also why time and again, we hear about organizations spinning off innovative units so that they can function outside of the stifling bureaucracy of the parent. But why not change the bureaucracy?

THE TECHNICAL SIDE OF BRAIDS

Braids operate as "socio-technical systems," not as social systems or technical systems in isolation from one another. People cannot do the work of knowledge sharing without the technology and the technology cannot do the work of integration with people doing their part. The social system and

Table 3.2.
Informal Components Of Braided Organization Design

INFORMAL COMPONENT	TRADITIONAL	BRAIDED
SELECTION	Match skills to job; secondary attention to cultural fit; "hire in"	Equal attention to capabilities and organizational fit; "buy-in"
TALENT PROFILE	Full time employment	Mix of full time, part-time, gig economy and robotics, AI
PRIMARY ORIENTATION	Individual achievement	Collaboration
PERFORMANCE ASSESSMENT	Individual	Team
CULTURE	Top-down; respect for titles; prescribed role and contributions	Shared responsibility; flexibility in roles and contributions; respect for person, not title
REWARDS	Primarily individual and extrinsic	Balance of team and individual, extrinsic and intrinsic
CAREER	Work your way up; seniority drives promotions	Develop broader capabilities by taking on challenging assignments; fewer levels mean fewer promotions; rewards tied to capabilities more than seniority
LEADERSHIP	Fixed, formal, command, and control	Representative, variable, informal, emergent depending on needs, peer to peer, consensus-driven
RULES	Rules proliferate and constrain behavior	Rules are minimized; those that exist are respected
TRANSPARENCY	Need to know	Open
PROCESSES	Mandated; penalties for failing to follow procedure	Codeveloped; viewed as essential to teamwork and performance

technical system are interdependent, as shown in Figure 3.2. One system can only work as well as the other allows.

Engineers and social scientists have examined the interface between people and technology for almost a century. Getting this interface right is essential to optimizing productivity, learning, and adaptability while minimizing costs, stress, and accidents. Understanding how people in braids interact with technical platforms and one another is critical to making them successful.

Technical systems (in this case digital platforms) are intended to ease or enable tasks performance. Organizational integration braids draw on digital platforms to accomplish a number of things that would be difficult or impossible for humans to do without their assistance (see Table 3.3).

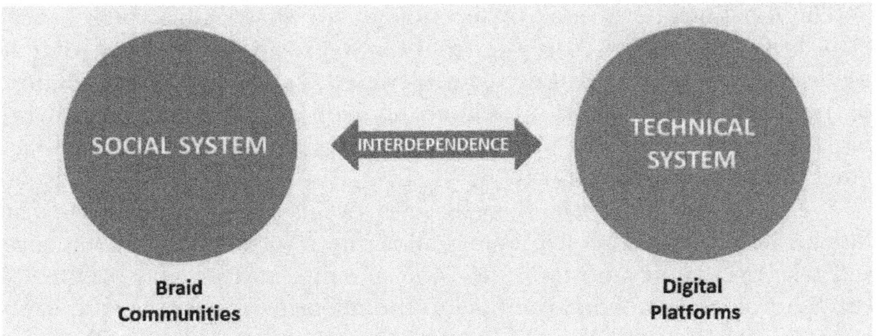

Figure 3.2. Integration braids as sociotechnical systems.

Table 3.3.
Functions performed by Technical Systems in Braided Organizations

TECHNICAL FUNCTION	DESCRIPTION
CONNECT PEOPLE	Connect people who would otherwise not be connected tightly or at all, enabling real time (chat) and asynchronous communication by using a variety of media across distance and time
COORDINATE ACTIVITIES	Coordinate project activities, track progress, identify bottlenecks, guide planning, trigger tasks, initiate corrective actions
COORDINATE PRODUCTION	Schedule production, track inventory, identify outages, monitor quality, identify critical path issues, conserve resources, optimize batch sizes
CAPTURE, STORE AND MAKE KNOWLEDGE AVAILABLE	Facilitate knowledge capture, retain knowledge in accessible data bases, simplify knowledge retrieval and application
SUPPORT DECISION MAKING	Predictive analytics, pattern recognition, risk assessment
MONITOR AND CONTROL SYSTEMS	Capture operational data for use in system control, preventative maintenance, automatic response, exception reporting

The functions performed by technology are what enable robust, powerful braids to exist. Before the technology provided by today's digital platforms, people were limited to restricted communications, reliance on personal social networks, backward-looking measures of productivity, nonsearchable databases, data-poor decision making, and after-the-fact emergency response protocols.

Even with advanced technology however, braids only work as well as their human designers and collaborators allow them to. Artificial intelligence will take over more and more decision making, and we may eventually reach a point where human inputs to the majority of decisions are irrelevant. Already, pundits are criticizing doctors who trust their own diagnosis rather than utilizing IBM's Watson to bring the latest medical knowledge to bear. While this may seem far-fetched or unwise, engineers at Schlumberger would be questioned if they made important risk-related decisions without tapping into the *InTouch* knowledge base. If you are going to build a powerful organizational integration braid, it makes sense to use it.

For now, and for at least a few decades to come, we humans still matter. Humans matter both in what they do (collaborate, consult databases, share knowledge) and what they *do not* do (keep up with the latest information, admit mistakes, make regular additions to the shared knowledge repository). In order for braids to work as intended, productive behaviors must be encouraged.

Douglas McGregor, in his famous work on theory X and theory Y that described assumptions that leaders hold about people pointed out that most people are naturally motivated to do a good job (McGregor, 1960). While correct as a blanket statement, it is not correct to say that people will always do what is right or that every individual will put the same amount of energy into trying. People come to work with a positive attitude and good intentions but sometimes encounter circumstances that make doing the right thing difficult. Such circumstances might involve a lack of training, inadequate tools, unclear objectives, negative peer pressure, an overload of work, insufficient authority, and improper incentives. We could label the sum of these circumstances "organizational culture" as long as we do not make the mistake of thinking of organizational culture as a thing that exists apart from its underlying determinants. If we think of culture as a stand-alone thing, we make the mistake of believing we can create it or change it simply by describing how we expect people to behave. Until we understand everything that is contributing to the culture, we will not be able to understand why the current culture persists even when we say very clearly that it needs to change.

The sociotechnical perspective helps us see and understand everything that explains why people are behaving as they are. People's behavior is a function both of who they are and what they encounter. When you think about yourself, who you are is a product of your beliefs, values, aspirations, upbringing, experiences in life, knowledge, relationships, emotions, abilities, and more. You probably think of yourself as a good person who is talented and capable of success in your role.

When you think of yourself at work, if you are honest, you might acknowledge that you have not always been 100% successful, mainly because circumstances did not allow you to be. You were not given enough time or information; people you counted on to do something did not come through; you ran into things that no one could anticipate; the systems you were using were poorly designed; your boss was a jerk; your customers' expectations were unrealistic; or perhaps you were just unlucky.

While you understand both who you are and what you have encountered, your judgment about others may not be as accurate. Rather than assuming that others are just like you (well-intentioned but not behaving perfectly due to circumstances) you attribute imperfect behavior on their part not to circumstances but instead to *them*. You see their poor behavior or performance as a function of their values, motivation, commitment, willingness to accept responsibility, being a poor team player, lacking sufficient intelligence, or not supporting the company line. Scientists call this the "fundamental attribution error" and we are all susceptible to it from time to time.

The reason why this is so important in understanding how braids work is that organizational leaders, and designers of the technical platforms than enable braids to function, frequently fall into the fundamental attribution error trap when observing that people are not behaving within the braid as they should be. If they are not contributing knowledge, or not tapping into the database, or not offering help to others who need it the automatic assumption is that there is something wrong with *them*.

In truth, because behavior is determined both by who a person is and the circumstances they encounter, it may well be that the digital platform or the organization itself is not designed to encourage productive braid behaviors. For example, while the success of the braid is based on the willingness of people to collaborate, they may be rewarded for their individual performance. Or, if promotions are awarded to people who hoard expertise and use it to make themselves invaluable, others will soon learn that sharing information freely is foolish.

Years ago, the designers of such things as automobile assembly lines and coal mining equipment discovered that they can engineer the technology so that it could run at a speed that was faster than human operators could keep up with. Today, digital platform designers are making the same kind of mistake. They are designing systems that could operate perfectly *if* they operated in a perfect world, where everyone was motivated to do the right thing, knowledge was uniformly distributed, barriers to applying knowledge did not exist, time was not a factor, and all information entered into the database was accurate and complete. Designers are ignoring the fact that braids are socio-technical systems, and that perfect technology will not operate perfectly if people are involved.

Braids do not have to operate perfectly in order to offer considerable advantages over non-braided organizations. One could say that the design of a digital platform is "good enough" if it provides a superior outcome to some alternative. This, however, would be like saying that a horse is a preferred mode of transportation compared to walking when an automobile or airplane is also available. If you seek the advantages that braids can provide, it makes no sense to design and operate them for minimal gain.

To obtain the full benefit of braids, it takes more than good technology. The organization must be designed to support and encourage braids to work as intended.

WHAT DOES IT TAKE TO MAKE ORGANIZATIONAL INTEGRATION BRAIDS WORK?

Figure 3.3 raises some questions leaders should ask when installing organizational integration braids. Each question should be followed by another: "If not, why not?"

If organizational integration braids are not working as expected, there is probably organizational design work to be done. To create a high-performance socio-technical braid, organizational structure, technology and the social system need to be aligned. Simply making available a digital platform is not sufficient.

All braids exist to connect capabilities, resources and opportunities, as indicated in Figure 3.4. The success of braids depends on how easily those with needs for knowledge/capabilities and resources can locate parties with capabilities or resources and thereafter form a relationship with them. Features of braids that make them more successful in accomplishing these basic purposes are shown in Table 3.4.

The function of the braid is to connect people who would like to be connected because their interests and needs are complimentary. It stands to reason that the braid should cast as wide a net as possible to find the best potential matches yet focus attention on the best "fit" matches that are found. If a party is not in the braid, the braid will not be able to facilitate the connection. Therefore, the *scope* of the braid is important, and more is better initially; but over time, a smaller set of the right connections are more easily coordinated.

We have been trying to get people to work more closely together across internal and external boundaries for a very long time. Now, we have tools

☐ Is the braid producing the expected outcomes?	☐ Are rewards tie directly to using the braid? To collaboration? To achieving outcomes that can only be achieved via teamwork? To contributing knowledge to the shared data base? To helping customers prevent problems?
☐ Are people collaborating using the braid? Are there tangible examples of the outcomes of that collaboration?	☐ Are barriers to accessing individuals and knowledge across units and geographies kept to an absolute minimum?
☐ Are there robust communities of practice within functions and representing critical areas of expertise?	☐ Are employees free to take actions that are necessary to address issues as they arise? Can they flex their roles as the work demands without having to seek permission?
☐ Are there knowledge sharing champions who facilitate access to digital knowledge management systems?	☐ Does the braid make it simple to access expertise and knowledge anywhere in the organization?
☐ Is the organization connected via strong social networks that cross functions, time and locations in order to support interdependent work?	☐ Do leaders encourage their people to use the braid and provide recognition when they do?
☐ Is the organization structured designed to enhance agility and minimize barriers to the execution of new strategies?	

Figure 3.3. Questions to consider in designing an organization to support work in braids.

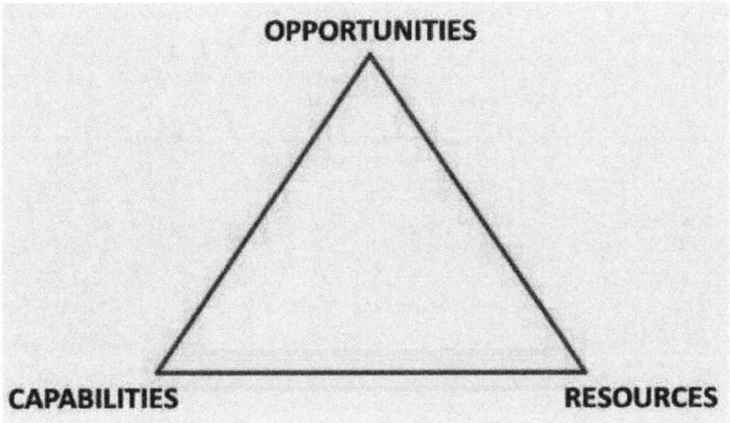

Figure 3.4. Braids act to connect opportunities, capabilities, and resources.

available that should make this easier than it has ever been before. In order to enable rich discussions and deeper connections, the ability of the braid to support a variety of forms of communicating (*multiplexing*) is a plus. Those of you who have used a conferencing service like Webex or GoToMeeting know the advantages that looking at the same picture while trying to share information helps greatly in comparison with the spoken word alone.

The *prominence* of the braid is important because the most prominent braids are the ones most likely to attract the people you would like to meet. *Algorithms* that help to assess the probable fit of potential resources can be developed over time to reduce the amount of time and effort expended that would otherwise be expended on failed relationships.

Table 3.4.
Features of Braids That Influence Their Success

BRAID FEATURE	EXPLANATION
SCOPE	When energy is available all around, the only issue is to be able to capture it. Plus store only the minimum vitally necessary.
MULTIPLEXING	The ability of the braid to support many different forms of data transfer and communication (verbal, graphic, text, video)
PROMINENCE	The potential of the braid to attract attention
MATCHING ALGORITHMS	The ability of the braid to screen potential members for compatibility using algorithms
STICKINESS	The ability of the braid to enable emotions to be conveyed in the service of creating better relationships
TRUST VERIFICATION	The ability of the braid to provide automatic referencing and assessments of trustworthiness
CONTENT CURATION	Content editing by a group dedicated to the truth and accuracy of material contributed by members of the braid
MEMBERSHIP CONTROL	Membership is curated to add quality while reducing number of low contributors
Diversity	In expertise, perspective, representation

Since braids are about forming working relationships among people, how you feel about another party matters. Is this someone I can work with? Will they be trustworthy, loyal, fun, energetic, responsive, or whatever it is that we value? If the braid enables the sharing of emotions (not just through emoji's, although it is a start!) it is more likely that good relationships will build momentum and investments in poor ones can be avoided. Since finding and deepening relationships is the purpose of braids, the "stickiness" of the braid, or the extent to which it attracts and holds attention over time, is a desirable feature. A stickier braid increases the number of opportunities for introductions to lead to continuing engagements.

So, it is with *trust*. Accommodating to the virtual world of braids means that you may never meet some of the parties most essential to your business. Since that is scary to anyone, the braid needs to provide independent verification that allows one to engage with confidence.

Content curation keeps trash from showing up on the screen, making the braid more efficient and more useful. It takes work to curate content however, so there is a tradeoff between ease of sharing information and the desire to make certain that the information is valid and useful. In the case of Linux, for example, anyone can contribute code; but the Red Hat organization gets paid by people who want to know that the code works and does not contain viruses.

An elite membership makes a braid more attractive while working against its scope. If Nobel scientists only want to discuss matters with other Nobel scientists, that is fine. If someone needs an answer that a Nobel scientist may not know, it is better to reach a wider audience. Nevertheless, given a choice, most people would prefer to be members of exclusive braids with *controlled membership* rather than braids anyone can join because there is a sense that the braid will be more efficient in producing relationships that are highly desirable.

Diversity is important to the extent that one seeks the broadest possible spectrum of expertise, perspectives, and alternatives. If we only engage with people who look, think and act like us, our views are reinforced rather than expanded. One of the true strengths of braids over face to face meetings is that we encounter the unexpected in so many different ways.

DASSAULT SYSTÈMES: AN EXAMPLE OF BRAIDED ORGANIZATIONAL DESIGN

Very few companies have experimented widely with braids as they are described in this book. Fewer still have designed themselves as braided organizations. While not entirely a braided design, Dassault Systèmes has been an innovator in the application of braids while still maintaining some aspects of more traditional organizing, and we use the company to illustrate how braids can complement and, in some instances, replace traditional organization design components.

Founded in 1981, Dassault Systèmes is a global software company based in France, providing 3D design and product lifecycle management (PLM) solutions for a wide variety of clients: aerospace and defense, energy, consumer goods, and finance among others. CATIA—Dassault Systèmes' flagship brand—is a world leader in 3D computer-aided product design software. Over its 35-plus year history, Dassault Systèmes has continuously transformed to stay in sync with the rapid changes of the high-tech industry and, critically, the accelerated disruptions, brought by ever-changing technologies, upon its customers. A spin-off from Dassault Aviation, the company established itself as pioneering product engineers. The company then successfully repositioned on the global market as an industrial R&D brand, enriching its portfolio via acquisitions of competitors and start-ups.

Building on its engineering and product development foundation, Dassault Systèmes continued reinventing itself to build a stronger focus on the customer while enhancing its commercial discipline. Expanding on its original emphasis on product and engineering process excellence, Dassault Systèmes focused on exceeding customer expectations by transforming their business experience.

Recently, Dassault Systemes has developed a unique, fully-integrated approach to managing the customer business, seamlessly connecting data, technology, and people on one common platform. This deep focus on what the customer needs today and in the future is contingent on real-time responsiveness to change. This enables Dassault Systèmes to endure the avalanche of disruptions, with all their unpredictable implications, which affect most businesses. "It is a core responsibility of the top management to connect the dots between 'what we do' and 'who we are,' " notes Laurence Barthès, the Chief People and Information Officer of Dassault Systèmes (personal conversation, Theano Advisors conversation with Laurence Barthès, 2016). "Each time our strategy is repositioned, we reshape our processes, organization and people. Holding a strong vision for who we are as a company, we are always open to change. Transformation is our DNA."

COMPONENTS OF DASSAULT SYSTÈMES' BRAIDED ORGANIZATION DESIGN

In the Core Work, Roles Trump Titles

In typical hierarchical organizations, job titles are used to determine and limit the perimeter of one's responsibilities. Titles clearly define one's playing field, position in the organization, and participation in tasks, decisions, and problem-solving processes. This strict specialization of resources via job titles enabled efficiency and productivity but made adaptation to change more difficult. In the new world, job titles can impede collaboration and productivity as they reinforce hierarchies, create departmental and managerial silos and prevent information from flowing continuously and swiftly across organization. Within Dassault Systèmes titles, while remaining on the business cards, take a back seat in the day-to-day work of the organization. The company has reinforced the concept of "roles" as the core organizing element for the structure and ways of working. Roles at Dassault Systèmes are *organization-agnostic*, meaning they are not associated with any specific departments or entities, and thus are "silo-free" constructs. Roles identify the potential contribution of individuals by defining capabilities and skills for each person within the broader organization. Roles are used to assemble project teams, matching project purpose and requirements to the competencies and skills of the individual team members. An individual can carry multiple roles depending on their skills and projects as well as the initiatives he/she is involved in.

Roles may evolve as new skills are added, but the initial repertoire of roles across Dassault Systèmes is defined by the company's top leadership. This more traditional top-down approach ensures a direct connection between roles and work people are doing and the strategy, business priorities of the company and the needs of clients. "Getting the roles right is an important responsibility for the top leadership. These are the building blocks for all of our teams. When effectively defined, roles enable us to assemble the best talents, with the most relevant capabilities for projects and initiatives we are undertaking as a company," explains Barthès.

Figure 3.5. Using roles rather than titles enhances collaboration.

In traditional companies, employees working for different entities with different targets and objectives often find it difficult to collaborate.

Boundaries established by organizational structure and budgets emphasize individual performance and territories, often create internal competition, frictions and the emergence of the "us-versus-them" mentality. At Dassault Systèmes, such counterproductive patterns emanating from traditional structure are prevented by design of roles, digital infrastructure, and internal ways of working.

When finalized, the "repertoire" of roles is shared among the entities who decide how those roles should be allocated (based on historical data and recommendations of the peers) and to which contributors within Dassault. People who fit the requirements are given that role for the year. As soon as a role is given to an individual, a virtual profile of that role is created on the digital platform (called the 3DExperience) and linked to the individual's profile. Via the platform, roles and contributors are linked to their respective teams, projects, and digital communities all managed through the same digital tools and spaces. Roles provide access to data and project management spaces and are also connected to the team's set of objectives, accountabilities, and timelines.

Typically, each contributor carries multiple roles, participates in transversal projects and is a member of at least one digital community. A structure based on roles allows for emergence of a different value creation process that is more agile and tailored to the real-time needs and dynamic objectives of the company.

UNITS: PROFESSIONAL COMMUNITIES OF PRACTICE

When an employee in one department takes on a new role, she or he automatically joins an informal community of professionals within Dassault Systèmes holding the same role but in other departments. For example, a product developer from the information technology organization automatically becomes a member of the same braid as another developer from the services or the R&D organization. Although each individual is working on different objectives and priorities, assigned by departments to which they belong, they automatically become part of the same braided team of peers that serves as a virtual 24/7 go-to support network for professional topics and other related challenges.

As such, contributors disconnected by formal organizational boundaries become members of one connected virtual structure, a braided community of peers, hosted on a common digital platform that enables communication, collaboration and continuous exchange. In contrast to the more traditional organizations, where boundaries and reporting lines must be respected and preserved, at Dassault Systèmes the emphasis from the top is on the "silo-free" exchange and information flow.

Employees are not only encouraged to interact across boundaries, but they are empowered by the leadership to do so freely, enabled via the available digital platform and technologies. "We must learn to work together with all players in our ecosystem. Faster. Alone we can't succeed. As leaders we must leverage and reinforce behaviors based on interactions within and across braided organizations and communities," notes Barthès.

INTERDEPENDENT PROJECTS

The 3DExperience business platform is the digital backbone for braided organizations. Designed to offer clients one-point access via a single interface to all Dassault Systèmes digital applications, it is crucial for a holistic and integrated business experience. The platform connects projects, processes, and teams across multiple disciplines and departments, bringing all of the elements to one place on one's desktop. The 3DExperience platform connects data, processes, people, and tools to enable real-time collaboration and a seamless project experience (see Figure 3.6).

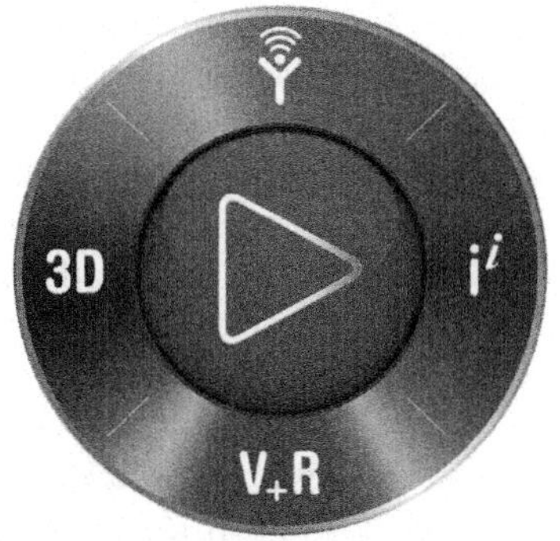

Figure 3.6. The Dassault Systèmes digital platform access page.

The same 3DExperience platform is utilized internally to operate most of Dassault Systèmes' internal management processes, and also to facilitate communication and collaboration between employees, customers and partners within Dassault Systèmes' business ecosystem. With just a few clicks the platform provides real-time visibility on the progress and milestones reached with specific projects, simultaneously integrating information from multiple sources. Provided the right level of access rights, one can tap instantly into the project dashboard (real-time metrics and activities) and logbooks (capture of exchanges and interactions) to learn about the evolution of the project, participation and contribution of members, profiles of individuals and partners involved, issues encountered, problems addressed and how those were resolved by the project team.

Since each individual collaborator experiences the organization differently, the 3DExperience platform provides each person with a customized view on the organization via a personalized view of the platform ("the personal window on the corporation"). Depending on her/his roles, the individual has access to different widgets or apps on the platform, to enable them to deliver on the projects. The individual dashboard reflects the collaborator's role(s), interests and networks. Just like braids, it is fully customizable and reconfigurable at scale.

ECOSYSTEM ACCESS

It is understood across the company that value can be generated from anywhere at any time. Value generation is no longer seen as a top-down concern, but as a shared, open and highly participative process that helps build stronger links between the purpose of the organization and its employees. Recognizing this as a core differentiator for the business and a booster of employee motivation and performance, Dassault Systèmes reinforces collective participation in value generation via its technology/platform and culture. Employees have an option of contributing to the business via the formal roles and processes or by voluntarily participating in braids. This emergent mechanism of value generation via the symbiotic, parallel structure of braids boosts the overall performance. The benefits of the braided structure are many, including these:

- ***Continuous exchange of information, data, and insights.*** Members of braids continuously share information, data, and insights pertinent to the purposes of their projects, products or initiatives. Insights are captured by the platform to be leveraged later or in real-time by other braid members. Continuous exposure and exchange of data and insights create a powerful information machine that enables decision making and better productivity.
- ***Fast resolutions of challenges.*** When unexpected issues or complex challenges arise, members of the braid can turn instantly to their wide network of peers for solutions; tapping into the collective brain while avoiding reinvention of the wheel.
- ***Idea generation and identification of opportunities.*** Frequent exchanges of experiences and knowledge between members from diverse parts of the organization and the broader Dassault Systèmes ecosystem facilitate the generation of new insights, unique ideas

and innovations with the potential to create new value and business opportunities.

- ***Effective collaboration and teamwork.*** Over time, members of the same braid develop strong social links and connections that help build trust and facilitate collaboration. Trust is an important catalyst for teamwork, especially among diverse populations and geographically dispersed, virtual teams.
- ***Professional development and growth.*** Learning from each other by sharing knowledge and professional experience through wikis, posts, and group chats, braid members develop much faster professionally. Often more experienced team members become mentors to their less-experienced peers, creating an environment of self-development and continuous learning.
- ***Engagement of individuals and teams.*** Being part of the same braid, sharing goals and a common purpose enhances the overall levels of engagement of people, and builds a stronger connection to the organization and its mission. Engagement impacts positively on employee satisfaction, retention, productivity, and therefore the overall performance of the business.
- ***Customer intimacy, satisfaction, and loyalty.*** Better customer centricity is achieved when more participants in the ecosystem of an organization gather and exchange data and insights on customer needs, issues, and preferences. A systematic exchange of customer information increase responsiveness to the evolving needs, and it creates a consistent customer experience across multiple touchpoints. Customer centricity correlates strongly with revenue growth and is a key factor in high-performance organizations.
- ***Better products and solutions.*** When harvested systematically by the organization insights, data and ideas generated via interactions and exchanges among myriads of braids within the company and its partner ecosystem, can be leveraged to improve the quality of products, offerings and processes critical to business success and growth.

DASSAULT'S INFORMAL SYSTEM

Strong purpose and culture are key to keeping a dynamic organization focused on the right set of priorities; such that everyone is marching to the same beat and behaving, collectively, in line with core values. At Dassault Systèmes the purpose of "providing business and people with virtual universes to imagine sustainable innovations, harmonizing product, nature and life" keeps everyone and everything in the company together. Serving as the "guardrails" to the nonstop flow of value-generating activities, the purpose guides people, teams and actions in the same direction with some boundaries. A lack of purpose and a strong culture would be dangerous for an organization that grows fast by acquiring and integrating many smaller firms, continuously enriching its portfolio and cultural DNA. "All must fit our purpose" is an unwritten rule that guides the everyday decisions on recruitment, hiring, promotions, and acquisitions. "Anything that doesn't fit with 'who we are' or 'what we want' to become is not accepted here," emphasizes Barthès.

Purpose is not a mere statement of intent. It comes to life through the performance management and talent systems, formal and informal organization, technology and internal infrastructure, as well as the portfolio of products, brand positioning and the platform. Braided, interconnected, integrated, continuous user experience is a new way of experiencing the business and the organization.

A strong culture is a major asset in navigating today's in-flux business environment. Building and nurturing a strong culture allows not only for leadership on the market, but also for more efficient operations and talents retention. One of Dassault Systèmes' key strengths is the powerful alignment between the components of its culture: its purpose, identity, values and methods. This continuous alignment is powered by the company's common denominator: the 3D Experience platform.

The company's purpose impacts its identity. Dassault Systèmes is a scientific and technological company that provides a portfolio of "Industry Solution Experiences," powered by the 3DExperience business platform, allowing businesses to simulate their end-consumer experience. To deliver on this promise, the company involves its customers and collaborators in the innovation process, through the platform.

Unsurprisingly for a software company whose performance depends on its intellectual capital, ability to transform and its capacity to anticipate clients' needs, Dassault Systèmes' key asset is its employees. This is reflected in the company's values, as shown in Figure 3.7.

Dassault Systèmes has a unique culture that allows for coexistence between traditional structure and braided organizations. First, there is a strong expectation of sharing data and working in a transparent way. Second, everyone is expected to proactively contribute to the evolution and the disruption of the company. Moreover, all the commercial, business and internal management activities are unified by one common purpose in line with the strategic position of Dassault Systèmes in the market. Finally, reconfiguration, adjustment, and change are the constants in the company's modus operandi and in its approach to management.

Figure 3.7. The company's values are positioned around a compass, identical to the navigation tool used to structure the 3DExperience platform environment.

Exposure and transparency permeate multiple systems at Dassault Systèmes. For instance, all the targets, accountabilities, project milestones, and performance objectives are uploaded onto the individual dashboards once roles are assigned and expectations for the year have been discussed and finalized. Contributions to projects, taskforces, and new initiatives are all tracked on the platform which feeds automatically into individuals' profiles providing real-time snapshots and visibility of all activities and contributions.

Aside from quantitative measures of performance, quality of contributions can be assessed, using the qualitative data and history which is also available on the platform. Managers can use the data to recognize people for their performance against the specific objective as well as for their participation and contributions to communities and partner networks. Of course, recognition by the employer has a positive impact on the motivation and performance of employees, who feel both appreciated and trusted by the company.

GOVERNANCE

Value generation is not a top-down process at Dassault Systèmes. It is distributed and shared among the population of contributors. People are empowered to take on new initiatives, and to address issues working directly with peers or even customers. There is implicit permission to hack—change, experiment, disrupt—the status quo, when needed. The culture at Dassault Systèmes allows individuals to engage in actions of "constructive deviance" if the objective is to improve the organization or generate new value. Anticipating that the formal decision-making and improvement processes will lag behind the speed of change experienced at the customer and market levels, Dassault Systèmes wants its employees to pick up the pace. Each individual within the larger "web of people" becomes an important sensor that inputs improvements and signals opportunities. Instead of waiting for the signal to reach the top and then for a decision to cascade back, employees are expected to take initiative—"personal leadership" as it is called at Dassault Systèmes—to tackle the opportunities. "This is the only way we can keep up with the evolution of the customers, the changes in new technologies—the only way we can stay relevant, at pace and agile."

Those taking on initiatives have a huge network of peers to rely on. Instantly, anyone with a good and relevant idea can identify other "like-minded" peers via the platform—connect, decide, and form a braid. The culture allows for this and the infrastructure enables it with just a few clicks. When the impact of such braids is positive on the performance of the organization, their efforts are recognized by the formal structure; they are scaled and integrated into the formal ways of working. Individuals and teams are recognized at company-wide events and similar behavior and initiatives are encouraged. When the organization puts in place processes for systematically harvesting such individually-driven initiatives, it creates a well-oiled insight machine based on the collective intelligence of its people (see Figure 3.8).

Figure 3.8. Like a spinning top, Dassualt Systemmes' organization structure is constantly in motion.

"MOBILIS IN MOBILI"

As the famous submarine invented by Jules Verne (1875), the *Nautilus,* which had the motto, "Mobilis in Mobili" moving in a moving environment, Dassault Systemes' multidimensional, hybrid organization is on the move. The combination of formal/hierarchal and braided—changing and adaptive structures mimic an environment and markets perpetually on the move. Complementing each other, the two symbiotic structures make the overall company both stable and dynamic. The formal, traditional structure makes the organization more stable and predictable, allowing for a clear focus on the core products, industries, customers and geographies. The braided part, on the other hand, makes Dassault more fluid and flexible, allowing the system to quickly change and adjust to keep up with disruptions in the environment.

This organizational ambidexterity—the ability to switch gear at runtime gives Dassault Systèmes a critical advantage. Resources can be identified quickly and reallocated to new projects. The best talent can be faster assembled into braided teams. The work of dispersed teams can be continuously supported by digital platform and tools seamlessly connecting data, insights, and people. A culture of change, experimentation, and the frequent shifts and disruptions create an employee experience that is appealing to the new generation of workers. Thanks to the ambidextrous organization structure in place the company can move much faster, matching the pace of disruption and external change.

At this point in its evolution, Dassault Systèmes has not abandoned more traditional top-down governance for a fully-braided representative approach to governance, as we see at Zappos or Mondragon. As long as its performance remains outstanding, we suspect that the combination of formal and braided ways of working will remain in place. We do not advocate full-braiding as the ideal solution for every organization. In many of the examples covered next, we see the application of braids in some parts of an organization but not others. What is right for your organization depends on both your readiness for braiding and the unique demands of your situation.

HOW TO DESIGN BRAIDS

To enable braids to work effectively, leaders and system architects need to envision the organization as it *should* work in the ideal. Then, they need to redesign the organization and systems that influence culture and behavior to support that way of working.

In general, organizations that are structured hierarchically and managed with systems that are intended to ensure control are the exact opposite of what is needed to optimize the kind of boundaryless, interdependent work that braids allow. Although in many cases braids will supplement the formal organization rather than replace it entirely, the formal organization can interfere with the effectiveness of braids. If organizations are designed with the kind of flexibility that Google or Zappos provide, braids encounter less resistance. If instead the formal organization dominates, people are not likely to take advantage of the power braids provide. Departments will remain siloed, information will stay hidden, and real collaboration will remain difficult.

Few leaders understand the nuances of organizational design and fewer still have had the experience of working in a braided organization. The world they know operates on a different set of principles (command and control) than those braided organizations require (trust people to run toward the challenges and to figure out how to meet them). Flexibility, continuous change and constant innovation are earmarks of organizations that are designed to profit from the implementation of braids. Actions needed to create the shift from a "braid-hostile" to a "braid-friendly" environment must be deliberate and far-reaching. Changing both the structure of the organization and its culture to support braids is necessary and doesn't happen without a comprehensive, integrated approach. It is extremely tempting to implement the infrastructure for a braid "in name only" over an existing organization and culture but this will produce incremental gains rather the desired effects.

As shown in Figure 3.8, to design effective braids, the process begins with determining what the braid is intended to accomplish. If organizational integration is the goal, what integration is sought and why is it critical to success? Who would need to be able to connect more tightly to whom? What would the specific goals of that connection be? From this, the next step is to clarify the goals for braid performance. Setting goals is important because they clarify the potential benefit of the braid and later serve as a dashboard to measure progress.

The next step is to envision the braid architecture as it should be designed. What data or knowledge needs to be collected, curated, stored, and shared? What communities of practice, functions, locations and individuals need to be connected through the braid? What decisions or actions would these connections produce? What authority would these decisions or actions require? What controls or quality checks need to be in place? What training and ongoing support would be necessary to animate the braid?

Then, with a rough idea of how the braid would operate, the organization architecture is examined to determine if the current structure and culture would enable or inhibit the braid's operation. This step requires an examination of the organizational chart, work processes, authority distribution, reward systems, talent, cultural diversity, leadership, and behavior. Experience in both organization design and working in braids is helpful in conducting this step. Since there is a natural tendency to preserve the status quo, an objective perspective is needed to see issues of alignment between the current organization design and the desired braid way of working. Leaders who have made the shift to braids at Airbus and Dassault tell us that it is harder than they imagined. Persistence over time is required. Instead of a "big bang" the reality of redesigning the organization to accommodate braids takes a good deal of commitment, trial and error.

Next, work on the technical aspects of the braid proceeds in parallel with efforts in organization design and culture change. On the technical side, a careful consideration of work requirements will determine which available platform should be used as the backbone for the braid or if an entirely customized platform needs to be developed. Platforms for integration, open innovation, and supply chain coordination have different operational requirements and demand different levels of investment in creating them, training people to operate them and maintaining their functionality over time.

Braid architects cannot design the ideal braid without help from people who understand the organization and its goals. Good braid design requires inputs from many sources, since what works in one location or one organization will not work in another. Iterative design processes test features as they are developed with a diverse community of potential users.

As the operational requirements of the braid emerge from the technical design process, they are fed back into the design of the organization's architecture. The architecture is composed of two elements; the formal organization and the informal system, or culture.

The formal system lays out how the organization is supposed to work in practice. Since people are used to working in traditional, hierarchical structures, explaining braids are supposed to work and how people are supposed to behave takes some careful thinking. As we will see, the organization chart may not look like an organizational chart at all, but a collection of circles of activities, indicating that collaboration is expected among people involved in the work. That work is what becomes "figural" while the kinds of reporting relationships that we find in traditional organizations, captured by organizational charts, fade into the background. People may "report" to many different "leaders" during the course of a few months, especially if they assigned to multiple projects. The concept of a single boss who provides day to day oversight doesn't really apply to braids. Instead, people work in networks that shift shapes depending on the work at hand (Johansen, 2017).

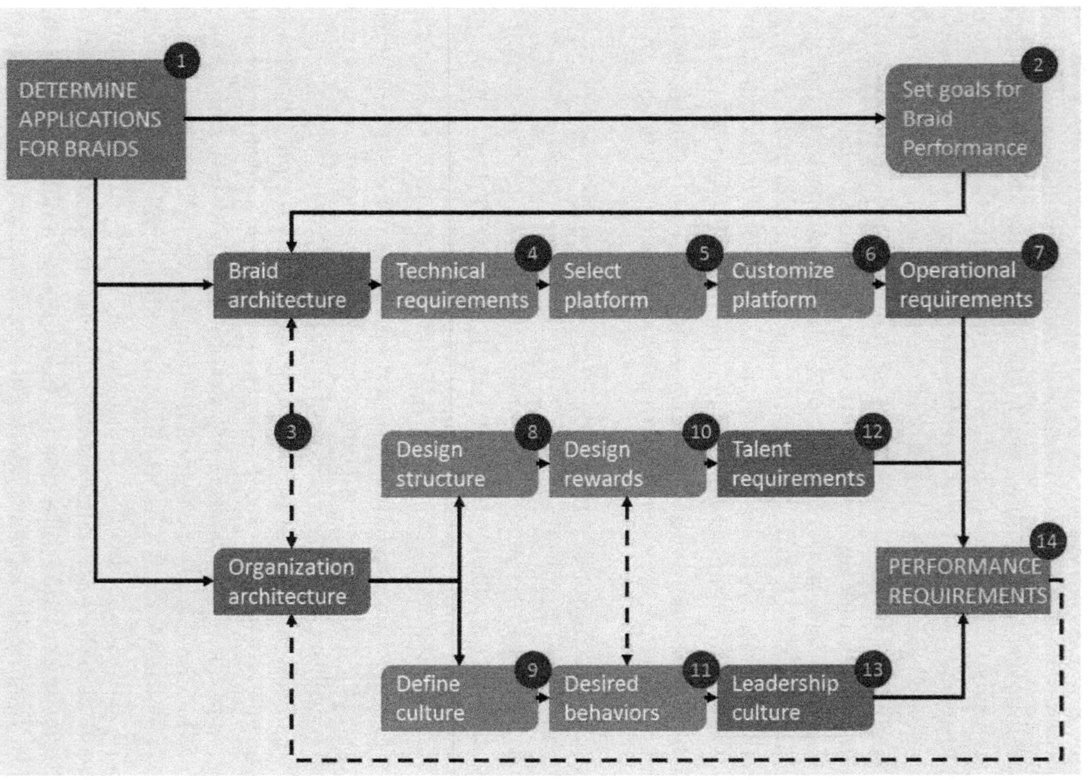

Figure 3.9. Aligning the organization to optimize.

Not visible in the chart but equally important are the processes that are to be followed to accomplish work within each of the elements of the organization. These processes can be loosely or tightly designed. Processes in one part of the organization can be extremely flexible and adaptive, while processes in other parts of the organization may be much more tightly constrained due to the nature of the work being performed.

Formal reward systems shape behavior by reinforcing efforts to produce the outcomes to which they are tied. While people may do the right thing regardless of how they are rewarded in the short run, in the long run rewards are one of the most powerful determinants of behavior (Kerr, 1975). Rewards should be designed to encourage collaboration in a braid rather than recognizing individual performance.

Talent specifications are another element of the formal design. As roles and responsibilities are defined, talent specifications should be aligned with the work that role-holders are expected to perform. Mismatches are not uncommon as people move up or around organizations but talent gaps across the board are a cause for alarm. Talent gaps frequently appear when new strategies or technologies are introduced. Training can help to close gaps but the replacement of talent in critical roles may also be required.

The informal organization is comprised of the culture and the choices that people make about how to behave. The informal organization can be described and influenced but not mandated or controlled. It has been described as "What people do when no one is watching." In Schein's (1985) classic formulation, culture is composed of artifacts, behaviors and values or beliefs. While artifacts like the arrangement of offices are easily changed, beliefs and values are much more difficult to reprogram. Usually, experimentation with new behaviors is necessary before people begin to shift their perspectives and adopt new beliefs or values.

Without direction, people will behave in ways that make sense to them given their historical predispositions and interpretations of what is expected of them. Rather than simply hope that people will do the right things to enable braids to work as intended, the desired culture and attendant behaviors should be carefully described and communicated. In addition, since leaders have such a profound influence on behavior in organizations, leaders should model and reinforce the behavior expected of others. As new behaviors gradually demonstrate their advantage, they slowly begin to take hold and eventually become "The way we do things around here." When leaders behave consistently in ways that support the organization's strategy, they create a *leadership culture* (McGuire & Rhodes, 2009). The leadership culture in turn shapes the larger organizational culture. We will discuss the leadership behaviors that are required to support braided working in Chapter 6.

The final step in designing braids is to install a measurement system that is intended to determine whether braids are producing required performance outcomes. The measurements should relate directly to the goals that were set for braid performance at the beginning of the design process. If the results are not as expected, investigation will reveal whether the design of the braid itself is at fault or the problem lies with interference from the organization's formal or informal arrangements. Rather than declaring braids a "failed experiment" leaders should be prepared to take steps that will enhance braid performance.

While designing and installing braids is not a simple or straightforward process, the outcomes can be well worth it, as we saw in Chapter 2. In the next chapter, we introduce some examples of where braids have been successfully applied.

CHAPTER 4

WHERE BRAIDS HAVE BEEN APPLIED

We now turn to applications of digital braids which are already amazing in their diversity and growing daily. As we shall see, the application of braids to a myriad of purposes is the equivalent of a new industrial revolution. What was once slow, difficult and expensive to achieve is becoming faster, easier and less expensive. These advantages will continue to drive innovative uses of braids in an even wider array of applications with advantages that we are only beginning to understand. Stand by for disruption.

ENTREPRENEURIAL BRAIDS

According to the U.S. Census Bureau (2017) in 2015, the nation's 414,000 startup firms created 2.5 million new jobs according to data from the Bureau's Business Dynamics Statistics. These young firms (those less than 6 years old) accounted for 11% of employment and 27% of job creation. Of course, startups aren't just important to the U.S. economy; we see interest in supporting startups as engines to fuel economic growth in both developed and developing countries around the world. Moreover, successful startups that have grown into huge firms can be found everywhere, from the U.S. to China, India, and Scandinavia. Think Wipro, Infosys, Alibaba.

Braided Organizations: Designing Augmented Human-Centric Processes to Enhance Performance and Innovation, pp. 71–104

LIFE WITHIN AN ENTREPRENEURIAL BRAID

Meet Eric Abouaf, hired recently by Theano Advisors to help spur innovation projects sponsored by the firm. Eric recounts his previous experience working in a small startup that was later acquired by a much larger organization, PagesJaunes, the French Yellow Pages.

Eric, then age 28, was hired recently by Theano Advisors to help spur innovation projects sponsored by the firm. Eric recounts his experience of working in a small startup right out of college that employed braids to its advantage.

> Antoine and I started thinking about forming the company in college in 2006 in a class on entrepreneurship. We were introduced to another friend who had an idea about building a system like the one that is used to make hotel reservations but instead that would enable people to make reservations on line for all kinds of professional services: doctor's appointments, getting your car serviced, beauty salon appointments and much more. I agreed to continue to work with Antoine and Eric to develop the idea further, not sure at first exactly what my long term interest would be.
>
> I decided to offer my development services in exchange for 15% of the shares in the company. After graduation, we founded the company officially and I became a 30% shareholder. We had no money at all. Antoine took out a loan for €3,000 and applied for and received a government grant for €6,000.
>
> We were living in Bordeaux with Antoine's mother. During this time, Antoine was meeting with doctors his family knew to test their interest in our online booking system. We weren't good salesmen, so we looked around for another partner who could help us. Antoine had someone in mind, but it turned out that he was a little older, had a young baby, and couldn't afford to take the risk. At that point, another friend of Antoine's, Guillaume, returned from India, where he had been selling wine. He joined us as an intern in 2007. Then, another friend of Eric's, Maxime, who was a year younger than we were also joined as an intern. He had technical skills but no knowledge of how to actually do application development.
>
> Here is when the braid began to build from the small intense group of the four of us to include others who would work with us to help us succeed. Guillaume started talking to potential customers; really, anyone who would listen: doctors, driving schools, beauty salons. We had the support of two coaches from our old school who had already started a business and knew what would be required.
>
> The Bordeaux region had a program that provided support for tech startups and they helped us develop a real business plan that we could begin sharing with potential investors. Beginning in 2008, we started pitching the company; we must have made forty or fifty pitches that year and we got better and better at doing it. The more we pitched, the clearer we became about the kind of deal we wanted to make with an investor. We

wanted more than cash in exchange for ownership; we wanted someone who was interested in helping to grow the operation. We found out that the maximum we could raise and still qualify for a government incentive program would be €500,000, so we set that as our target. In 2009, we settled on an investment group from the Versailles region, where there were many high-level executive contacts. Our primary partner was a former CEO who contributed €460,000 and another angel investor who brought €50,000 and also ran an online business. We wanted to learn everything from our investors that we could, although in the end, it turned out that they couldn't help us as much as we initially thought.

With the money we raised, we went from four to ten employees and forming some outside partnerships. We needed web developers, phone counselors, and customer support people. We found it difficult to attract older employees, so most of us were in our mid-twenties.

Our customers helped us a lot. The chief marketing officers of larger clients required a lot of attention and a professional attitude. We could wear casual clothes when dealing with some customers but for others, we had to put on suits, which made us a little uncomfortable.

We participated in a number of conferences and trade shows where we learned what others were doing. We found it easy to engage in dialogues with other companies who wanted us to use their platforms, like Yahoo. Google also helped. They had no browser then but were pushing hard to enhance the web and using it to store data offline in the event that internet services were lost, which happened a lot back then. We freely exchanged information with competitors; we were small and growing but not a threat to most people. Some competitors were specializing in applications for the health care industry because it was a big potential market. We decided to remain broadly focused. We did fear a competitor that was being sponsored by Orange (the phone company) but when we saw their application a year later we knew it was terrible and would never sell.

We partnered with a small website developer to help us with our portal. Small businesses were building their own websites and online booking solutions so we learned from them more about what the market needed. We were looking for a larger partner who could help us grow faster and thought that the ideal partner would be PagesJaunes. Fortuitously, they called us first. One afternoon, Antoine came in saying, "You'll never guess who that was—it was PagesJaunes and they want to buy us." They saw us as a good fit with their core business and wanted to buy us outright rather than invest in us as a separate entity. We knew we needed a transfusion of cash to build out the app. We decided to sell but remain on, working for PagesJaunes.

When we joined PagesJaunes, the organization had not fully transitioned to the digital state. There were 8,000 people with a paper-printing mindset. We were culturally different. To help with the transformation, the company sponsored a series of braids and you could decide which to join.

I joined the data braid, which was called a "User club." The startup workshop had 35 people, the next 20. The initial workshops were face to face. Our goal was to write white papers to share best practices in data analysis, then act as evangelists on what we should do.

Management was really pushing the user clubs. There was a project called "Digitas 2016." There were no specific goals; the user clubs chose their own topics. Management supported the user club meetings but couldn't follow much of what we were recommending. The business rationale wasn't always clear. They saw some of the ideas as dreams that wouldn't add business value. Most of the user club members were from subsidiaries rather than regular full-time employees. Still, people did become better connected which was a major accomplishment.

We then had 'make it days' for some of the ideas coming out of the user clubs where the focus was on making something tangible that could be taken to market. The idea was to be able to build it and ship it in three days. You didn't sleep for 24 hours. It was like a hackathon. Another organization I know of called it "FedEx days" but then had to change the name.

We selected three ideas for funding but there wasn't an incubator infrastructure, so things didn't move smoothly. One leader launched his team's idea secretly just to avoid interference from other leaders from finance and human resources. Their involvement would have put more conditions on the work that would create obstacles. It would have killed the excitement.

A board was created for each of the projects with people mainly from the subsidiaries rather than the main organization. Our little subsidiary was left to operate independently within the larger organization. As projects became visible it became more challenging because it takes time to integrate the ideas with the rest of what was happening and bring them to full fruition. Most of the new ideas extended the scope of the organization rather than threatening existing jobs.

We found that even with just 30–40 people, you need common technological platforms that allow braided interaction. We used Confluence and Salesforce platforms to run the company. With Confluence, we asked every employee to contribute either by writing about something they knew or asking about something they didn't know. We put all our meeting reports into the tool. We had a global space and one for each team. In one month, it became the way we worked; we no longer used email. We'd put the agenda up and then allow people to comment on it; after the meeting, we made notes and others could read about the meeting. This platform is really for discovery. It's a small world where you can navigate the organization. Confluence also worked well with the other tools we were using for data management and project management. We had a lot of online tools. Most of the business was run on Salesforce but Confluence was the place to start and learn how we did things. It would teach people how to use Salesforce, for example.

In larger companies that use Confluence, the tool tends to get used within teams rather than on a larger scale. It should be able to be put to larger use. The company that built it is using it with about 2,000 employees. You can search for the names of topics you wish to find so that you can connect. Someone starting a braid can post an invitation to others.

PagesJaunes started all the user clubs at the same time with an email to all employees. When we use agile technologies, there is always a coach.

Open source software has changed the way we work. GitHub is where designers share their code. Anyone can publish source code in the wild so that others can find it. Anyone can change it as they wish. We can also send a "pull" request to the people who owned the code so they can choose to incorporate the changes into their work. Even Facebook has offered a lot of open source code. They get value because we extend it and improve it. People publish solutions. In my small company, we needed a way to customize forms for every single customer; we put out a request for solutions to the community and by the time we had the app, it was done. Usually, the people who share solutions are not direct competitors but they could be. We put a lot of R&D time into creating something that the CEO didn't want to share. I know that our competitors wouldn't have used it, but other kinds of companies would have. These are tough decisions.

Facilitating this kind of interaction among people who you don't even know to connect to is critical to forming braids—and cheap. Open source is always a balance between competitive advantage and taking advantage of the knowledge that is out there. Facebook doesn't "sell" what people post; they make their money elsewhere. These systems are working against years of traditional ways of working and structure."

Clearly, the work that is going on at PagesJaunes is different than what anyone working there 10 years ago could have imagined. Eric is only one of hundreds of young entrepreneurs who were invited to join the organization to play with ideas that could add new dimensions to the company's business model. Not every user club produced ideas that added immediate value. Still, it is hard to conceive that the same innovative work could have been accomplished by existing groups of employees pulled together into a task force, committee or action learning team. New perspectives are more apt to come from fresh eyes using new ways of working.

On reflecting on how the braid developed in Eric's small startup and then in the larger PagesJaunes organization, Eric realized that the braid was important from the very beginning. Even though the core braid at the start was a very intense face-to-face collaboration between two people and then four, it quickly expanded to include helpful customers, advisors, supporters and investors. Figure 4.1 captures how the braid evolved.

At first, it was a couple of guys with an idea living at home to conserve funds. Early on, discussions with potential customers helped shaped the direction the startup took. Then a few more college acquaintances joined, bringing capabilities the original partners needed. As the idea took shape and a few early customers came on board, the partners were able to raise funds, hire more people and connect to more people with capabilities that were essential for growth. Once acquired by PagesJaunes Eric and his partners started using digital platforms like Confluence to manage the company and connect them to resources and knowledge they required.

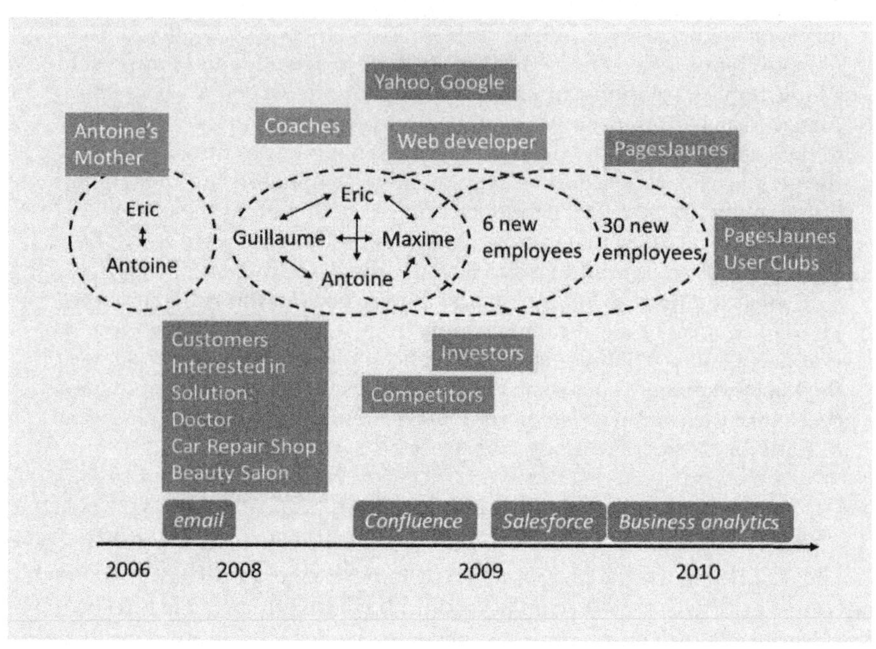

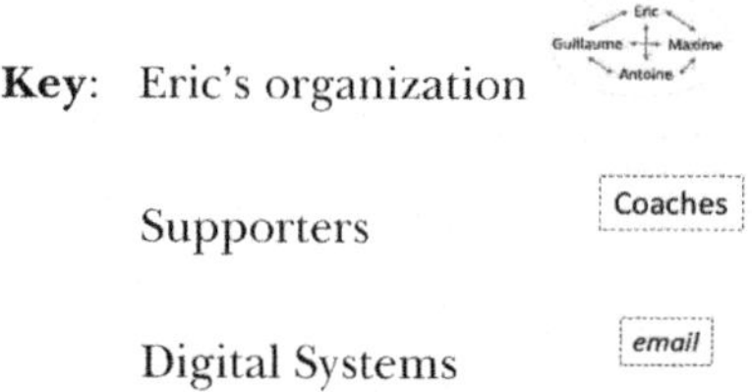

Key: Eric's organization

Supporters

Digital Systems

Figure 4.1. How Eric's startup braid evolved over time.

As Eric's case shows, the classic image of the one inventor working in his or her garage for years on end to bring a closely guarded secret to market is giving way to a different approach, one supported by braids. Rather than working alone, with only the knowledge and resources immediately at hand, today's entrepreneur has access to help through braids. Entrepreneurs operate both outside of formal organizations and within them. Support and knowledge are available in either case, from different sources. For the organizational entrepreneur, day to day survival issues are not a worry. Still, accessing available knowledge and speeding ideas to market can be facilitated by tapping into external braids. For individual entrepreneurs who seek the big prizes of creating their own company or cashing out on a disruptive invention, braids can increase the odds of success by providing funding, technical knowledge, marketing expertise and business advice.

The creation of braids has made the work of entrepreneurs easier, faster and more successful. Just as it is easier to find new knowledge using a Google search than it is to go to the public library, entrepreneurs don't need to struggle nearly as much to find what they need. Of course, not all ideas are good ideas and the reaction of parties in braids will help entrepreneurs find out if their ideas are worth or unworthy much more quickly than in the past. To say that braids have "super-charged" entrepreneurship would not be far from the truth. Entrepreneurs of the future will still work in garages and basements at times, but they will be much better connected to the outside world. Entrepreneurship is an excellent application of braids, as Eric's example demonstrates; but big companies are interested in starting new businesses as well. Sometimes, this requires that they take steps to disrupt their own business before others can. Some are employing a fairly new approach known as "Disruption labs" that combine braid-working with hackathons to produce innovative business models.

INNOVATION/DISRUPTION LABS

Disruption labs raise the stakes one notch higher than incubator braids. Their charge is to disrupt the industry before others can do so. Some organizations are sitting ducks. They have no clue what is happening in the world around them and don't seem to care. They are shocked when their business model is disrupted and due to their lack of preparation, too slow to adapt to survive.

A second group of organizations are watching what is happening around them anxiously but still hopeful that disruptions won't affect them, at least until they can figure out how to respond. Some hope to be acquired while others may retreat to a defensible niche where revenues and employment are much smaller but sustainable. They become boutiques and cede the field to the innovators.

A third group of organizations is not content to let the future determine their fate. They go out to create the future they wish to inhabit. Peter Drucker (2014) once famously said, "The best way to predict the future is to create it" and that's exactly what these organizations intend to do.

Either you are committed to disruption, or you are not. There are so many pressures to play it safe, provide fallback alternatives, or fail to make the really big moves that it weighs down innovators like chains around their ankles that will not allow them to soar. Cutting the chains, which involves letting your current investors, supporters, employees and customers know that you are about to head in a new direction, means risking that you could lose it all. So-called "wise" advisors would say that one should place incremental bets until the virtue of the strategy is proven; and in most cases, that advice would be sound. However, if true disruption is the goal, incremental does not work because each step does not go far enough to produce a truly new way of working and with each small failure that is encountered along the way, the advice is to pull back rather than find a way forward.

WalmartlLabs (walmartlabs.com) has as a mission redefining e-commerce globally. Even for an organization as large as Walmart, that's an audacious goal. Statista (Statistia.com) estimates the global e-commerce market will grow to 3.4 trillion U.S. dollars in 2019. That's a lot of business. Like many big box store retailers, Walmart can see the future and thinks it will need a stronger e-commerce channel to fend off Amazon, Google, and other competitors in the evolving global market for groceries and consumer packaged goods. Walmart's recent purchase of Jet.com, a fast-growing online retailer for 3 billion dollars was a step in the right direction but only a start. Simply having an e-commerce website will not be sufficient; Walmart already had that before acquiring Jet.com. What Walmart will need is breakthrough innovations to change how people shop.

Google is already expanding its home delivery of groceries and Amazon Go offers shoppers who still like to shop in stores a hassle-free shopping experience. Using "smart-shelf" technology, customers simply collect the items they want and walk out of the store; the shelves do the work that cashiers used to do. Customers can monitor how much they are spending on an app on their mobile devices. Amazon also purchased WholeFoods, a high-end largely organic food chain in the U.S. but it is not clear yet how online and in-store shopping will evolve under Amazon's ownership.

The goal of Walmartlabs is to expand the number of ways that Walmart customers can shop at Walmart and make those shopping experiences as simple and enjoyable as possible. Taking full advantage of braids for open source innovation, Walmart labs hosted a "WMTCode hack" at TechCrunch's #HackDisrupt in which 600 programmers used Walmart's Application Programming Interface (API) to offer suggestions about ways Walmart could offer new shopping experiences. In these sessions, teams have 24 hours to come up with ideas, so no one sleeps. The time pressure of the "sprint" is part of the fun and what makes hackathons successful. The winning team invented a way for people to use their smart devices to locate any item in a given Walmart store, making shopping more efficient. It was a cool idea but only the beginning. There is much more that will need to be done to change the way people shop. The goal is to provide alternatives, so that people can shop in the way they prefer, which maximum ease and enjoyment. Already, almost half of shopping occurs online, a phenomenon we could not have imagined 20 years ago.

Walmartlabs describes itself as an innovation engine within a large corporation. It is a different kind of entrepreneurial braid. Because most of the work is done through the application programming interface, hackathons can take place simultaneously on a global basis, with teams inspiring ideas in other teams. Walmartlabs itself is headquartered in San Bruno but also located in a number of locations within the United States (including at Walmart's headquarters in Bentonville, Arkansas) as well as in locations offshore (India, London, and Brazil). Being a part of a global entrepreneurial community built with the intent to disrupt Walmart's way of doing business for the better is a powerful attraction to the young, talented people who join in the fun.

Besides Walmart, many other "traditional" companies have opened units that are dedicated to disrupting current business models. They locate these units in places like Silicon Valley, Bangalore, or London where digital communities exist that promote innovation and commerce. The reason for this is not only that the culture at headquarters is bureaucratic and traditional but that the digital community is elsewhere. People in Silicon Valley, Bangalore, Boston Tel Aviv, and London are gathering to live the digital, entrepreneurial life and often move from company to company or startup to startup because the opportunities are attractive. In the process, they get to know one another, personally or virtually. This enhances the exchange of information and reinforces the belief that innovation is not only possible, it's happening.

After opening seven innovation labs across the world (see Figure 4.2), Bank of New York Mellon—a global investments services and investment company with $30.5 trillion assets, has recently established its eighth innovation center in Singapore—the capital of FinTech and innovation technology. The ambition for these labs is to bring together a "team of teams," or a *superbraid* as we would call it, to collaborate, create, and accelerate data-driven market solutions and innovations. The braid composed of more than 100 engineers across the world is exploring disruptive technologies such as IoT, Big Data, Cloud, and blockchains to build insights, develop new capabilities, better catering to the rapidly evolving needs of their clients. "BNY Mellon is a technology company that is cleverly disguised as a bank," said the Managing Director of the labs Michael Gardner.

JP Morgan Chase, a competitor of Mellon, has assembled a team of 50,000 technologists to rework existing processes but also break new ground, creating its own cryptocurrency to enhance the security and speed of transactions (Hackett, 2018). Lori Beer, CIO, describes the organization as a "digital bank powered by a leading technology company." To encourage innovation, the bank created its own disruption braid, called "New Product Development" where people interested in working on cloud computing, digitization, machine learning and APIs could find a comfortable home (see Figure 4.2).

Source: BNYMellon "Global Innovation Centers" report 2017 https://www.bnymellon.com/us/en/_locale-assets/pdf/bnym-globalinnovationcenters.pdf

Figure 4.2. Mellon's global disruption projects.

MetLife—the global life insurer, is another example of a traditional player that has been very proactive in disruptive thinking. Its LumenLab, also based in Singapore, hosts innovation resources (experts with prior experience in other startups, labs and incubators) dedicated to identifying new sources of value for MetLife. The mission of the LumenLab is to lead from the front the innovation for the life insurance industry, serving the MetLife's business value creation engine, sourcing disruptions and identifying new business models for existing markers.

In terms of the structure, the lab is comprised of not only the dedicated internal experts but also members from the external community, for example, the National University of Singapore, the Economic Development Board and Monetary Authority of the state-island (see Figure 4.3).

One of the recent successful innovations by the LumenLab is the quiz app called BerryQ *(*see Figure 4.3*)*. Its purpose is to increase the overall health and wellness awareness among its users. The app asks and answers

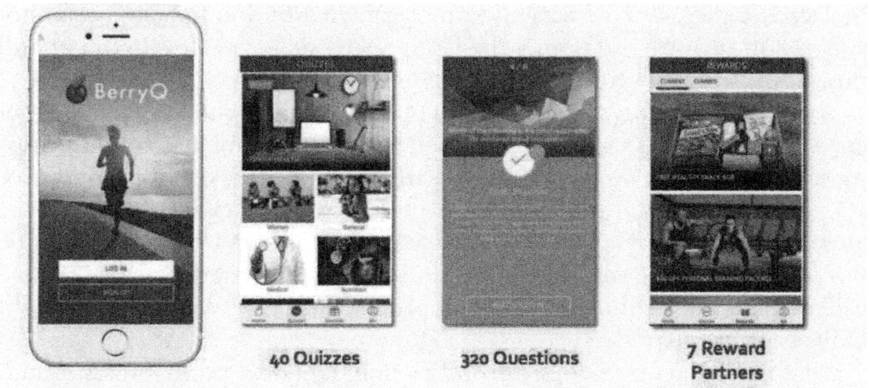

Source: Metlife/Lumen Lab website BerryQ http://lumenlab.sg/2018/02/10/berryq/

Figure 4.3. MetLife's Berry Q app.

questions regarding a variety of health and wellness topics including nutrition, stress, and even traditional Chinese medicine. Based on responses to multiple choice questions, BerryQ provides a personalized overview of the users' health awareness, giving practical tips, and rewarding for higher health literacy scores. One of such rewards is a free annual membership for the Urban Remedy—a local fitness community.

ConVRse—is another innovation targeted for the India market. In essence it is the first virtual reality (VR) customer service technology applied in the life insurance sector. This VR technology and device allows customers to interact with a virtual MetLife customer service expert—an avatar called Khushi—in a virtual environment to receive personalized service and to address questions regarding the policy and its requirements. For a company that is nearly 150 years old, these experimental and game-changing projects are critical for MetLife's continuous transformation and survival.

In a converted warehouse in San Francisco, Sephora—a beauty giant, is housing its dedicated to disruption Innovation Lab. Established to reimagine the future of shopping experience for Sephora's 10.6 million customers, its aim is to integrate both the digital with the in-store retail experience. Although the purpose of the Lab is simple "to ideate, dream, experiment, and test new offerings," the pressure on the company to successfully innovate is high; LVMH the parent company sees Sephora as its primary growth vehicle.

In spite of its small size the Sephora braid dedicated to self-disruption, about 10 people, knows how to leverage the broader network of contributors from within Sephora and externally within its ecosystem of partners. Programs such as Idea Central and Think Tank have been put in place to "cull the collective creativity of Sephora's 14,000 employees," notes Calvin

McDonald, the CEO for Sephora Americas. In addition to being the innovation and disruption engine, the lab is also a space for development and growth of Sephora's future digital leaders.

As the lab continues to operate, the portfolio of Sephora's ecosystem of apps and services is expanding. Now it includes a number of mobile apps providing tutorials on applying makeup products (Pocket Contour, Color IQ, and SkinCareIQ) personalized to each user's specific face shape, the augmented reality displays featuring women founders of various cosmetic brands available at the store, and a membership-based delivery service called Flash that competes with Amazon Prime in 2-day and overnight delivery of cosmetics.

When internal knowledge is insufficient to fuel disruption, organizations may look outside for help. Braids can help form and support relationships between ideators and organizations that produce powerful partnerships.

OPEN INNOVATION: RESEARCH AND INNOVATION BRAIDS

It is truly amazing how time flies. The 1970s brought us the first cell phones and earliest personal computers. The 1980s the Internet, the space shuttle, and compact discs; the 1990s, Linux operating systems, HDTV and eBay; and the 2000s, the iPod, iPhone, and Kindle. The 2000s, a decade that is just a few years behind us, also brought something that today, like these other inventions, we now take for granted: open innovation.

By the year 2000, P&G's innovation success rate, despite spending billions, hovered around 35%. After missing Wall Street estimates that year, P&G's stock plummeted from $118 to $52, costing investors more than half the company's market capitalization. In order to produce the 4–6% organic growth that was needed to restore the company's value, P&G would have needed to build the equivalent of a new $4 billion dollar business in a year—a tall task by any standard. Faced with this challenge, P&G did what few organizations would do at the time; rather than plow more cash into internal R&D, they asked for help from the outside.

Charged by P&G's then CEO A.G. Lafley to reinvent the company's innovation process, Larry Huston, Vice President for Innovation and Knowledge and Nabil Sakkab, Senior Vice President for Research and Development, scoured academic journals, attended conferences and benchmarked other R&D organizations to find a breakthrough. Having read hundreds of the latest books and articles on R&D productivity, they concluded that what they were looking for did not exist. They would have to invent it. Studying the success of a few products brought in from the outside, Huston and Sakkab realized that there were smart people outside of P&G, not just within its own R&D facilities. In fact, while there were 7,500 P&G scientists at the time, Huston and Sakkab estimated that there were around a million and a half scientists and engineers outside P&G who could be called upon for help. The light bulb went off and "P&G Connect and Develop" was born (Huston & Sakkab, 2006). Lafley soon-after mandated that fully 50% of P&G's innovations should come from outside rather than from within. A change in culture was required to make this happen, which was not easy in an organization full of prideful superstars and a strong track record of success. Had Lafley not been insistent, Connect and Develop would have never taken hold. Olay Regenerist, Swifter dusters and Crest spinbrushes were early wins, providing the additional revenue that P&G sought to meet its growth targets. With success and strong support from the top, doubters were silenced.

Today, open innovation is taken for granted by many companies as a supplement to internal R&D efforts; yet few have practiced it with P&Gs conviction or success. While the concept seems like it would be easy enough to grasp, implementing it is harder than one might imagine. At the time, for example, the digital network of over 700,000 external scientists P&G wanted to target did not exist; so P&G had to help create it (it was called "NineSigma").

Unlike Lafley who initiated open innovation at P&G, Jim Whitehurst inherited one of the world's leading open companies, Red Hat. Red Hat owns and operates the Linux computer operating system which has, since day one, operated as an open platform to which users can contribute. To learn more about this model of running a company, you can click on opensource.com, a website created by Red Hat as a service to the world that shares insights from the experience of working and leading open source communities. You'll find articles like "How to build your code club on GitHub" and "Get emotional: Tips for open source communities." Or you can read Jim Whitehurst's (2015) book, *The Open Organization*, which tells the story of Whitehurst's journey as the CEO of Red Hat and talks extensively about how Red Hat operates as a company. We will return to that in discussing leadership in braided organizations later in the book. For now, we're interested in using Red Hat as an example of how you can build a company valued at over $10 billion dollars by letting others do most of the work.

Whitehurst (2015) makes the advantages of an open organization clear in the following passage.

> An "open organization"—which I define as an organization that engages participative communities both inside and out—responds to opportunities more quickly, has access to resources and talent outside the organization, and inspires, motivates and empowers people at all levels to act with accountability. The beauty of an open organization is that it is not about pedaling harder, but about tapping into new sources of power both inside

> and outside to keep pace with all the fast-moving changes in your environment. (Loc 170 Is this a page number?])

Sounds great. But how do you do it?

The essence, according to Whitehurst (2015), is crowdsourcing to communities of highly motivated volunteers. These are people who care about the challenge in question and derive tangible or psychological rewards from the opportunity to be a part of what we would call a braid.

Whitehurst (2015) notes that to sustain the community indefinitely, both the host organization (if there is one) and the members of the community must perceive that they derive value from their participation. Prizes or incentives offered to volunteers can produce short-term interest but will not sustain ongoing participation. At the core of most open-source braids are a few individuals who may not be on anyone's payroll but keep the attention of the braid focused on the right challenges and moving ahead rather than constantly starting from scratch. If the braid is initiated by an organization interested in open innovation, the core group will include some company employees. Over time, others will join and some of those people will take a more central position, either because they enjoy working on the challenge or they find ways to profit from their contributions.

At Red Hat, Linux was created by an open source community that sought an alternative to Microsoft and other proprietary operating systems available on the market. The motivations for joining the Linux community were diverse. Some wanted to add features that were not available in existing operating systems. Others wanted to be free of the charges that existing operating systems extracted from users. More than a few enjoyed the challenge of writing cool code and being part of a very smart community of peers who understood and appreciated their creativity.

The network provided additional critical advantages. When bugs were encountered, or new capabilities were needed, the community could respond immediately. There was no need to wait for the next "release" of a proprietary operating system to see if the bugs had been addressed or the capabilities you need had been added. Speed and adaptability to solutions were much greater. The more time people work in the braid, the better they understand what is going on. As a consequence, they can generate more ideas of interest to others and do so more quickly. As the braid expands, it adds capabilities over time. This increases the motivation of members to stay in the braid as well as to add their own contributions so that others will be motivated to stay in the braid as well. It is to everyone's mutual benefit to help one another out. Unlike in proprietary operating systems, the ideas that rise to the top are not those that management deems the most important. Instead, they are the ideas that meet the needs of community members and do so in the most efficient and elegant manner.

Some time ago, we worked with a major consumer products company's research organization. We noticed that a large portion of the scientists were not very positive about the prospects for success of the projects they were working on. We thought that odd at the time, since these were extremely bright people hired from the best schools and capable of making significant contributions. When we dug deeper, we found that the reason for the rampant despair was in the way that decisions were made about which projects to pursue. Instead of using the combined brainpower of the organization, the organization operated in a hierarchical fashion. People needed to wait until they were promoted to a management position to be granted the power to decide which projects to undertake. Once they got there, they were eager to start working on projects they were longing to pursue. Junior scientists were expected to accept these decisions without question until it was their own turn to lead.

How different is this from the open innovation braids at P&G and Red Hat? Night and day. P&G's Connect + Develop open innovation system attracts scientists from all over the world to contribute to P&G projects they want to work on; no one is "told" what to do. Members of the Red Hat Linux community don't even wait to be invited by Red Hat to work on a particular fix or upgrade. They decide among themselves when and where to apply their skills.

At P&G, the path from open innovation to revenue is clear. The company solicits input on projects it has considered but also welcomes ideas from others. Thousands of ideas are offered, from which P&G commissions the contributors to pursue further work on those that appear most promising. Both P&G and the Connect+Develop community share the benefits of P&G's open approach to innovation. Dupont, 3M, and Kodak use similar models for open innovation.

At Red Hat, the connection between the open source coding community and profit for Red Hat is not as obvious. Since the Linux operating system is free to users, Red Hat does not profit from user fees as do the owners of proprietary operating systems. Instead, Red Hat makes its money by working with companies who use Linux or other Red Hat systems and are willing to pay for Red Hat's expertise. These companies need to be able to trust that the software will work properly and know who to go to when it does not. While each enterprise using Linux could simply throw out problems to the Linux community to solve, they feel more comfortable knowing that Red Hat people, who are intimately familiar with the code and work with the community on a regular basis, are guiding them. Whitehurst uses the analogy of water; we could simply go to a swamp to find free water, but we prefer to buy branded water in a bottle because we trust that it will be pure and safe.

Henry Chesbrough is a leading researcher on the subject of open innovation (Chesbrough, Vanhaverbeke, & West, 2006). He and his colleagues define open innovation in the following way: "Open innovation is the use of purposive inflows and outflows of knowledge to accelerate internal innovation, and expand the markets for external use of innovation, respectively."

There are a few important things about this definition. First, the flow of information is *purposive*; it is not a random sharing of thoughts or family pictures like one would find on Facebook, Snapchat or Twitter. Second, information flows two ways; both from the members of the community to the community or organization, and from the community to the participating member. Both directions of communication are valuable. The member contributes to the knowledge of the community and extracts knowledge from the community. The purpose of open innovation communities is to invent things of use, whether within the community or across a broader population. It takes the combination of these characteristics to inspire members to join an open innovation community and to maintain the community over time.

To benefit from the innovation that occurs, an organization like P&G or Red Hat needs to understand what the community is doing and how the innovation can be applied. Chesbrough calls this ability the "absorptive capacity" of an organization. To create absorptive capacity, investments in R&D or smart people who can decipher the chatter that is taking place are essential for success. However, staffing the organization for success at open innovation isn't as straightforward as it sounds. Why? Because open innovation leads to opportunities that may not fit the company's historical focus or business model. Truly new to the world innovations that require entirely fresh ways of operating may be difficult for an existing organization to assess or accept. This issue is at the Core of Clayton Christensen's work on barriers to innovation in large, established companies (Christensen, 1997). Our biases affect what we see as relevant, useful, and attractive for further exploration.

P&G and other companies have experimented with roles for people whose job it is to scan the environment for useful ideas. Some organizations, like Becton Dickenson, the medical products company, have sent people to places like Singularity University in Silicon Valley to take up residence for an extended period. Singularity teaches leaders about the technology of the future but also runs an ongoing incubator, in which innovators receive support from Singularity and one another.

Regardless of the approach used, what is important is that an organization that sends people out into the world be prepared to listen to them when they return. Singularity University reports that some of its resident executives have had difficulty influencing their parent organizations upon return from their extended stays. It is one thing to experience the "vibe" of the valley for oneself and another to have it described for you by someone else.

To counter this inherent NIH (Not Invented Here) bias, as we noted previously, a number of organizations have set up disruption braids in Silicon Valley, which provides a natural open innovation neighborhood. Xerox was one of the earliest to do so. The lessons learned were twofold; open innovation can be extremely successful but may not benefit the host organization if that organization lacks absorptive capacity. Xerox PARC (Palo Alto Research Center) produced wonderful innovations, but Xerox didn't benefit from the investment nearly as much as others, like Apple, who immediately saw the value in what Xerox PARC was doing. So, here is the point: It makes little sense to go to the trouble of crowdsourcing solutions, setting up roles for innovation scouts or creating entire innovation units if no one is listening. One end of an open innovation braid connects to the outside world; but the other end must connect to the host organization and do so effectively.

Some executives new to the open innovation process have the mistaken notion that because open innovation takes place outside of the organization, they do not need to be involved. They imagine that the call for help goes out and solutions come floating back in, ready to put on customer shelves. Reality is not that simple. Innovations cost time and money wherever they come from. The same amount of effort that it takes to go from innovative idea to commercialization on the inside has to be given to making an open innovation effort successful.

It follows that to do the work of open innovation, a structure with the right roles, staffing and budget is required to translate external ideas into valuable products. As companies gain experience with open innovation, they go through the maturity curve shown in Figure 4.4

In the beginning, open innovation is treated as an anomaly; something to experiment with, but not in a big way. Expectations are low, as are investments in the activity. A person is usually assigned to manage a single partnership or a small network of outsiders who are paid to produce ideas. The organization prioritizes its own innovations above those from outside. Open innovation composes a very small portion of all new products or services.

If early open innovation efforts are successful or the need to increase investments in open innovation becomes apparent, the early stage model is replicated on a larger scale. Instead of a single partner or a small network of contributors, multiple separate initiatives are undertaken simultaneously. These efforts compete with one another for continued funding, but are still prioritized lower than internal innovation efforts. Open innovation is responsible for less than half of the new products or services brought to market.

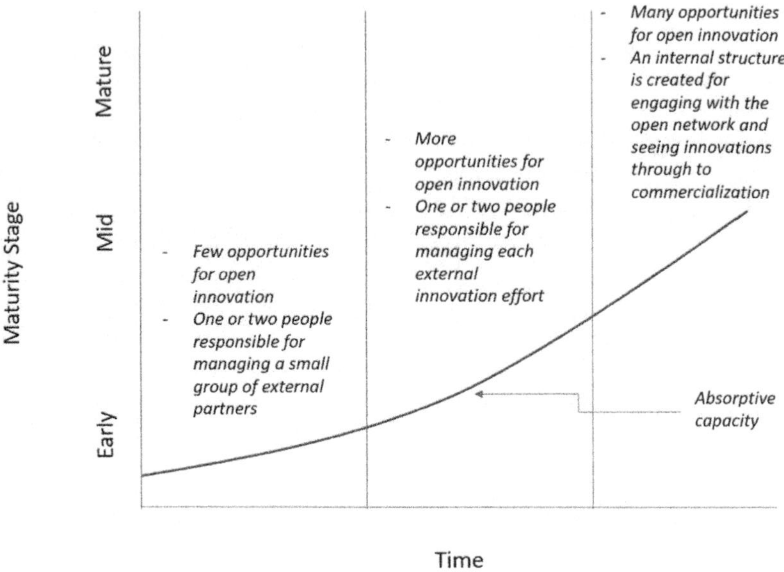

Figure 4.4. How internal structures evolve as open innovation efforts mature.

In the mature stage, the business model and culture around open innovation has shifted. Open innovation is recognized as a dynamic and powerful source of marketable ideas. A structure is created that fully supports the exploration, early innovation, and commercialization process for ideas from the outside. The structure has many points of interface with multiple external partners and/or a large, digitally-supported internal-external innovation braid. Open innovation efforts account for more than half of the organization's new products or services.

As indicated in Figure 4.4, the absorptive capacity of the organization grows over time. This is the result of a number of factors interacting simultaneously. Early experiences with open innovation produce learning about what success requires. The right actions need to be taken to set open innovation into motion and the natural forces of inertia, like prioritizing internal innovation over external innovation, must be overcome. With success comes confidence and greater investments. More people in roles devoted to making open innovation successful make influencing decision-making easier than it was when one or two people had to carry the responsibility alone. Once structures are put in place, the process of open innovation becomes easier, increasing its success. Investments in structures, systems and processes make collaboration in the braid easier, increasing the attractiveness of participation to external entities. With a larger, better connected and more successful innovation network, people are more inclined to get and stay involved, even in the face of challenges. Momentum builds along with success. Confidence in open innovation grows, as does absorptive capacity.

Some organizations abort their open innovation efforts in the early maturation stage because they don't produce outcomes of value. It is now easy to understand why achieving success with open innovation is a process that takes investments over time. In the case of P&G, Lafley acted as a resolute champion through the early and mid-phases of open innovation. Now having attained the mature stage, P&G is reaping the benefits of the investments made. It would be interesting if P&G could calculate the return on investment of open innovation compared to what it would have cost to do the same work internally; obviously, there's a strong belief that open innovation is the better strategy.

PROJECT/ORGANIZATION INTEGRATION BRAIDS

Necessity is the mother of invention. Schlumberger, a company we introduced earlier, is a global oil equipment construction, engineering and installation company that really needs to have its act together. Schlumberger is the world's leading provider of technology for reservoir characterization, drilling, production, and processing to the oil and gas industry. The company employs more than 100,000 people representing over 140 nationalities and working in more than 85 countries. With 125 research and engineering facilities worldwide, Schlumberger invested $1.1 billion in research and engineering in 2015. The price of learning how to do what the company does is enormous, as is the cost of repeating a mistake. For business as well as ethical reasons related to safety, Schlumberger must "know everything that Schlumberger knows" and "apply everywhere what we learn anywhere." Schlumberger has worked hard to create a knowledge-sharing culture. A number of digitally-supported braids link employees within the company, as well as connecting Schlumberger experts with customers seeking information (Stahl & Buckles, 2016).

Many organizations understand the value of knowledge-sharing and take steps to encourage it. Over 80% of the world's largest companies have some kind of platform for collecting and making available important intellectual property to increase efficiency, improve problem solving, accelerate training, avoid repeating mistakes, and improve customer response time. According to the *Oilfield Review* (2016), Chevron has reported that its system has saved the company over $2 billion annually Grant (2013).

Few organizations achieve these kinds of savings because they do not invest properly in developing robust digital platforms or the organizational cultures required to capitalize on them. For Schlumberger, making these investments was a priority given the nature of their business and the risks and benefits involved. The basic tasks involved in creating a highly-functioning organizational integration braid are listed in Table 4.1.

For Schlumberger, there are multiple benefits of building and maintaining an organizational integration braid. Mistakes are avoided, solutions are generated anywhere in the world more rapidly and at less cost, people share knowledge more readily, and service can be provided to customers who seek a long-term partnership with an organization that maintains an up to date repository of critical operational information.

Table 4.1.
The Basic Tasks Involved in Creating an Effective Project/ Organizational Integration Braid

Task	Description
GENERATE KNOWLEDGE	Whether through research or actual project work, create knowledge that is useful and therefore inherently valuable
CAPTURE KNOWLEDGE	Using various media (documents, graphics, videos, formulas, training manuals, etc.) record knowledge that has the potential for reapplication and store it in an accessible location
CATALOGUE KNOWLEDGE	Develop a system that allows knowledge to be curated, distilled, indexed and made searchable for easy retrieval
SHARE KNOWLEDGE	Design, build and populate knowledge management platforms with information to make it easily accessible; the platform should enable effortless collaboration between individuals and teams in creating solutions
APPLY KNOWLEDGE	Encourage awareness of the existence of knowledge that has been captured and encourage its widespread reuse; assist in the application phase by providing expert support
ENFORCE QUALITY	Verify that the knowledge stored in the system is high quality, up to date and easy to apply
OPTIMIZE ACCESS	Information must get to the right people at the right time while protecting intellectual property and data security
ALIGN WORK PROCESSES	Processes and supporting systems must be introduced that integrate work across the enterprise, allowing interdependent action (organizational integration braids)

To make this possible, the organizational integration braid has to be designed, built and operated for success. The old IT saying, "garbage-in, garbage-out" applies here. Just as devastating are behaviors that undercut the effectiveness of the braid: not capturing data, not accessing the data base when creating solutions, not taking time to help those who need your expertise, not updating the knowledge base when information becomes obsolete, and being so protective of intellectual capital that customers cannot benefit from its application. These issues are not technical, they are cultural. Schlumberger had to invest energy in changing its culture so that the integration braid could achieve its goals.

Schlumberger began work on its braid around 1996, considerably ahead of many others. It first built an intranet for the company that could serve as a connector and provide a hub for knowledge distribution. At about the same time, it began developing standards for knowledge capture and sharing. This greatly facilitated information exchange across functions and around the world. Some companies make the mistake of allowing units to invest in local solutions for knowledge sharing and integration. Schlumberger recognized that allowing different units to have their own systems would impede the organizational integration they sought.

Over time, Schlumberger developed thousands of searchable web pages for different kinds of knowledge applications and user communities. The InTouch application and Expertise Directory allow Schlumberger personnel to not only find the expertise they are looking for but to know more about the personal lives of the people with whom they are collaborating. This allows people to connect at a deeper level as opposed to simply sharing technical information. These deeper connections support more robust collaboration, spurring people to offer help without being asked, check up on how things turned out and stay in touch as new knowledge is generated. Schlumberger has learned that effective organizational integration takes more than connecting people to information. It requires connecting people to people, and people to communities of knowledge, in real time. Only then can the information be used effectively to achieve business outcomes.

Building out its systems, Schlumberger added decision support tools and simulation capabilities that allow teams to test solutions before putting them into practice. Today, the Schlumberger hub and specialized portals for different areas of expertise allow quick access to knowledge by different functions and communities, including marketing, research and development, field operations, finance and human resources. It is significant that the organizational integration braid at Schlumberger was designed to bring down the walls between all of these groups rather than being focused on engineering knowledge alone.

Full organizational integration, as is possible in the Schlumberger braid, permits human resources professionals to help put in place appropriate reward mechanisms that encourage information capture and sharing and track their effectiveness. Finance can help with tradeoffs in the costs of different customer solutions and make pricing information more accessible at the time that bids are being prepared. Marketing can leverage information about the nature of customer inquiries for expertise and anticipate customer needs before they become a source of concern.

Eureka, Schlumberger's portal for technical excellence, allows the "geeks" in the company to contribute to a shared knowledge base which can be easily interrogated. When expert interpretation is needed, the platform helps connect people directly to the contributors of knowledge or to their peers. Using the MindShare tool that Schlumberger created, project teams can access project archives and work collaboratively on projects in real time, capturing essential project-related information as they go.

A recognized group of over 300 knowledge community champions capture best practices and assist others in learning them. Help is also available through help desks that assist those who are having difficulty locating information they need. Today, there are more than 75 help desks that provide 24 X 7 service, staffed by more than 165 full-time engineers. When requests come into the system that are novel and require solution generation, these solutions are then pushed back out to users who have "subscribed" to that area of interest.

The information in the company's intranet-based knowledge management system is put to double use in training company personnel. It is used by instructors and incorporated into distance learning modules that people can access from anywhere at any time. The goal is to provide just-in-time education to increase the quality of learning and reduce wasted expenditures on long classes at training centers where information taught is not easily retained.

The Schlumberger organizational integration braid has saved the company billions of dollars since its inception, cut the time needed to resolve technical queries by 95% and reduced the workload needed to update engineering modifications by 75%. It has helped the company predict and thereby avoid risks in drilling and exploration, strengthen customer relationships and streamline bidding and contracting processes. Just as importantly, it has helped create a unified, knowledge sharing culture that could not exist without the digital tools and common standards that are at its core.

SUPPLY CHAIN AND ECOSYSTEM BRAIDS

Braids are the essence of modern supply chain management (SCM) as the complexity and global reach of many supply chains makes rapid coordination among diverse entities both challenging and vital. Despite national boundaries and contentious politics, supply chains are a force for global unity; supply chain expert John Gattorna refers to them as the "Independent Republic of Supply Chain." Keeping agreements knitted together and goods and payments flowing freely between customers and suppliers is what supply chain braids are all about.

Because the costs of supply chain failure are extremely high in terms of missed revenues, lost customers and damaged corporate reputations, it is not surprising that braids emerged as solutions early in the world of supply chains. Long before the existence of digital backbones to manage supply chain relationships and orders, the human aspect of supply chain braids was already operating. The Egyptians, Greeks, Romans, Dutch, and English all developed elaborate trading routes based on trusted relationships with far-flung partners. Accounts were kept, goods were shipped, and customer orders fulfilled. These basic functions are still performed today, but at a scale, speed and degree of complexity that early traders could not have imagined.

Today, we view supply chains as more than warehouses and fleets of delivery trucks. The modern, expanded view of the supply chain extends from the raw material suppliers to other suppliers, inbound logistics, internal operations, outbound logistics, distributors, retailers, customers and ultimately product recycling or disposal. This "cradle to grave" perspective has been adopted because an organization cannot optimize its supply chain unless it can influence every aspect of it; knowing what's on hand in the warehouse is no longer sufficient to meet the vagaries of customer tastes and demand. Because the market for goods and services is constantly shifting and evolving, organizations feel the pressure of making more rapid, frequent, and significant changes in supply. Supply chains have gone from being relatively predictable to extremely dynamic, increasing the emphasis on rapid interactions and adjustments among interconnected parties in response to self-induced innovation and external disruption. This is a job for braids.

WalMart is well known for its supply chain prowess, but so are Apple Dell, IKEA, Unilever, and Airbus. Supply chains are the front line for competitive battles that will determine who earns the right to continue serving customers in a world where costs, quality, speed, customization, sensitivity to the environment, concern for human rights and service are easily rated and compared.

Winning supply chain battles and ultimately the competitive war requires constant aligned innovation among multiple parties who themselves have both shared and competing agendas. For example, the same suppliers may serve multiple competing customers. Depending on their relative power, suppliers can push their customers to provide more attractive terms with regard to pricing, delivery, larger, or longer guaranteed orders and so forth. Since individual interests can sometimes work at cross-purposes with overall supply chain optimization, there is more to supply chain management than using sophisticated algorithms to calculate the economic order quantity. There are human negotiations that constantly take place as massive data analysis programs spit out instantaneously updated information about everything from sales to commodity prices to predictions about the impact of the weather. These negotiations occur with the help of braids.

Airbus, the European manufacturer of airplanes, is a victim of its own success. As a result of successful designs and a proven track record, the demand for its latest model aircraft, the A350, has, pun intended, skyrocketed. With orders coming in from every corner of the planet, Airbus did what most businesses would probably do; accept them, knowing that there would be challenges in meeting the demand that would need to be worked out.

The increase in production targets alone would have a huge impact on Airbus's supply chain partners. The equipment needed to manufacture the parts that make up the extra planes did not exist in the quantity required. In fact, parts suppliers lacked even the floor space to house the new equipment; new facilities would need to be constructed. The capacity for shipping wings and engines from where they are built to the final construction facilities would need to be augmented, which in itself would be a challenge. Across the supply chain, additional personnel would have to be hired and trained. At the final assembly plant, more space, more labor, and more equipment would be needed. To coordinate all this, an enhanced digital backbone would need to be built to allow communications to flow freely between hundreds of suppliers, so that every single part could be tracked as required by regulations and the planning of production could be optimized.

Adding to this complexity, one reason for Airbus's recent success was its willingness to allow customers to design cabin arrangements and decorating to their unique specifications. This meant that aircraft meant for different customers would have different parts and different suppliers.

Combined, the pressure to ramp up production and also customize the product led to an overload of the existing supply chain's capability. At a time when mutual coordination and problem solving was most needed, managers of facilities began to make independent decisions. If they couldn't do everything that was being asked, they would do the best they could, using their own judgment. As it became increasingly obvious that delivery commitments would not be met, Airbus leaders knew that action was required to address the situation; the problems would not solve themselves.

Part of the solution was strategic; tough decisions would have to be made about how many aircraft could be delivered and by when given the data that was becoming available about the real capacity of the supply chain. Second, actions would need to be taken to increase the capacity of the supply chain, in a coordinated way that engaged suppliers in planning for the future, making required investments, and improving manufacturing processes. Airbus needed to break down the wall that existed between the organization and its suppliers. Instead of using threats to force suppliers to comply with new requirements, Airbus became a partner in helping suppliers plan for the future. Supply chain experts from Airbus strengthened the digital backbone that managed the supply chain and worked on the human interactions within the extended supply chain braid. Leaders in the middle of supplier organizations who were close to the work were given voice, so that issues could be brought to the attention of Airbus and resolved. When unexpected problems were encountered, they would be made immediately visible instead of hidden as they had been in the past.

While Airbus couldn't avoid scaling back deliveries in the short run, the results of the crisis were a more realistic approach to supply chain planning and a more coordinated, participative approach to supply chain management. This strengthened braid will serve Airbus well going into the future.

At GE, the manufacturer of jet engines and gas turbines, the recognition that suppliers need to be tied in more closely to manufacturing has led to the creation of braids which are called "digital threads" as described by Steve Lohr (2016) in a recent *The New York Times* article:

> In the past, a model of a new part would be made and then converted to detailed blueprints running to 70 pages or more. These would then be physically sent to G.E. manufacturing engineers and outside suppliers to begin setting up the tooling, casting and cutting for the part.
>
> This prototype-and-blueprint routine took up to eight weeks. Now, engineers use 3-D computer models, skip the prototype step and instantly send the models electronically.
>
> This goes a step beyond computer-aided design, which is commonplace. In Greenville, the designers are for the first time linked directly with manufacturers and suppliers in real time, in what G.E. calls a "digital thread." This means they can collaborate in ways that have changed the work process while making it more likely that problems or defects are spotted sooner.
>
> Traditionally, one set of engineers designed a part, and only then passed it on to manufacturing. If a problem arose on the supplier side, the design was kicked back and the process started over. "Jobs are combining in this digital world," Mr. Lammas said.

GE's digital threads are built around its Predix platform. GE has used its Greenville, South Carolina factory where gas turbines are built as a test-bed for Predix. The interactions between suppliers and GE engineers are shaping the way that Predix can be used to help supply chain partners anywhere form digital threads that use data to more quickly spot issues and inform decisions, beginning with design and flowing through manufacturing, in-field monitoring and across a product's life span.

Once these kinds of supply chain braids become more common, the current scenario involving intermittent communications across siloed entities will seem antiquated and ludicrous. WalMart, beginning in the late 1990s, encouraged major suppliers like Procter & Gamble to assign full time staff to live at WalMart's headquarters in Bentonville, Arkansas to enhance communication and collaboration with their WalMart counterparts. But even physically locating supplier representatives on site cannot accomplish what braids will allow. Armed with instantaneous data regarding production and consumption of goods on a global scale, decision makers can more rapidly understand what is selling and what is not, try experimenting with new product designs or formulations in different markets, understand the impact of changes in packaging, see the effect of targeted marketing campaigns, more quickly replenish stock in preparation for discounted sales, and in many other ways act as if the entire supply chain was a single entity with a single brain. The technology to allow this level of coordination is not the barrier at this point; it is understanding what to do with the capabilities the technology provides.

Discovering the promise of braids will require new ways of working and thinking. Cultures that emphasize keeping business decisions secret, maintaining a separation between suppliers and customers, and working within one's own organization instead of with people from other organizations will need to give way to more collaborative cultures. Leaders, individuals and teams who once sought the "one right way" to do things will need to adopt more flexible mindsets that constantly search for new opportunities for improvement. Returning to the GE example, Lohr (2016) captures this insight from the head of engineering at the Greenville plant:

> Yet in Greenville, engineers in the design stages are encouraged to move faster in smaller steps, conduct more experiments, and be willing to fail and try again. It amounts to a sea change in the engineering culture of heavy industry.
>
> "As an engineer, not getting it right the first time, I find painful," said Bill Byrne, an engineering manager. "It's uncomfortable. But it's been incredibly liberating."
>
> The old ways, said Mr. Lammas, the engineering chief, had merit. Each step and rule was logical on its own. But the emphasis on flawless execution and perfection fostered a fear of failure. "Overcoming that culture was probably the biggest challenge," he said.

The old assumption was that the buyer had the technical expertise and final responsibility to make the final decisions regarding product specifications and supply chain design and operation. The new assumption is that as full partners, suppliers have as much right and responsibility to improve products and supply chains as buyers do. What is best for the whole is best for each of the parties involved. Over time, as the parties continue to work together and to learn as braids make more knowledge available, their operations should co-evolve.

As the Airbus example indicates, the notion that supply chains are made up of independent entities that operate at arms-length is untenable in a world of rapid, unpredictable change that requires efficient, coordinated responses. Braids provide the social and technical connections that enable much faster adaptation to occur.

For Airbus, the challenge was primarily to use braids to tie existing suppliers together more tightly and to react to issues more quickly. For other organizations, where products and services are evolving rapidly to keep up with technological advances, new software applications, or shifting consumer tastes, the challenge is to find new suppliers quickly and integrate them into the existing supply chain system seamlessly. The shift from building in-house production and logistics capabilities to outsourcing and off-shoring has been dramatic as organizations seek to optimize returns on capital, avoid long-term capital tie-ups and stay focused on the work that they can do uniquely well.

Fourth party logistics providers, joint service companies and virtual networks have emerged as the latest models for logistics outsourcing. These new alliances entrust external firms, partners or providers to build supply chains and create the digital backbones that allow them to operate. Gattorna (2015) defines a Fourth Party Logistics Provider as "a supply chain integrator that assembles and manages the resources, capabilities, and technology of its own organization with those of complementary service providers to deliver a comprehensive supply chain solution" (p. 462). In stepping back to see the expansiveness and complexity of global supply chains, it makes sense that independent organizations like SAP and UPS would evolve the expertise required to construct and operate effective supply chain braids.

Often, the culture required to operate more resilient and sustainable supply chains in a world of increasing complexity and threats simply is not part of the host organization's DNA. Yossi Sheffi of MIT suggests that fully flexible supply chains require a dynamic culture characterized by:

- Continuous communication among informed employees
- Distributed power
- Passion for work
- Conditioning for disruption

These essentials, we would argue, can be met by the formation of robust supply chain braids. When Boeing set out to build the revolutionary Dreamliner, it also took a leap forward in the way in which it managed its supply chain. Instead of owning and controlling the various elements that would comprise the supply chain, Boeing elected to distribute the costs and risks among partners. While sensible and futuristic, Boeing's decision at the time was not supported by an investment in supply-chain-coordinating braids. The lack of such braids caused delays at Boeing in dealing with supply chain disruptions. These well-documented disruptions in delivering the Dreamliner cost Boeing shareholders almost a third in returns during the period; that amount of money could have covered the costs of building a more resilient and dynamic supply chain management system.

Of course, investing in strengthening supply chain braids is a little bit like buying insurance; until there is a disruption, you do not believe you really need it. The cold truth is that the majority of organizations do experience supply chain disruptions (one study in the U.K. suggested as high as 88%) and given the growing complexity of supply chains and the level of economic, political, and environmental turbulence, the future portends that supply chain failures will become much more common.

Working against disruptions is the power of big data and analytics; real-time information processing on a massive scale, with point of manufacture and point of sale data allowing predictive analytics to be more readily available. As we get better at formulating data analytic services, supply chain leaders will be able to take action to prevent supply chain disruptions before they occur—providing that supply chains are sufficiently braided to allow directives to be put into action by parties up and down the supply chain.

In many organizations, there is a mad dash to acquire the talent that will enable big data analytics systems to be devised and supply chain coordination to occur. Because the market for truly top-level analytic talent is extremely tight, organizations will face the choice of making do with less than they need, seeking help from analytic and supply chain service providers, or turning to external braids to get the help required. Given the pace and complexity of change, taking the slow road to developing internal expertise is likely to cause organizations to fall farther behind if they don't complement that strategy with some form of talent acquisition, whether it be permanent or temporary. What is absolutely unacceptable is to stand still, betting that no investment in increasing analytical and supply chain coordination capabilities is required.

Some organizations solve the analytics talent problem by acquiring other companies with expertise or being acquired. While acquiring or being acquired may make sense strategically, leaders of combinations continue to underestimate the difficulty of aligning systems and cultures after mergers. Estimates by McKinsey and others indicate that the overall failure rate of strategic combinations continues to hold at around 70%. Clearly, buying or selling supply chain capabilities is not a panacea.

There is no shortcut to building resilient, adaptable and sustainable supply chains. The required actions in Table 4.2 must be taken, whether through internal development, acquisition, or utilizing external services. Many of these actions could be aided by the creation of digitally-enabled supply chain braids.

Table 4.2.
Issues in Supply Chain Design That Can Be Assisted by the Formation of Braids

Issues in Supply Chain Design That Can Benefit from Braids	
Action	Definition
Supply Chain Alignment & Integration	Creating digitally enabled, trust-based connections among all parties that permit rapid effective adjustments to shifts in demand including product design, quantity, and timing without the need for excessive discussion or re-negotiation among parties
Predictive analytics	In order to minimize the risk of severe disruption and to optimize overall supply chain efficiencies, big data analytics are developed that point toward changes in demand, supply or requirements and enable parties to adjust in anticipation of potential shocks instead of following them
Flexible supply chain models	Designing supply chains to operate under different business models that don't hinder adaptation to emerging competitive situations or local market variations
Dual mindset culture	Managing the "costs vs. capabilities" polarity; both are required but each necessitates a different mindset and culture among supply chain leaders and partners
Customer influence	Gathering data from customers and with customers to better understand what customers need today and want tomorrow and how they are reacting to innovations in products and services; bringing the customer into front-end design processes; helping customers formulate solutions to their challenges; increasing the intensity and value of interactions with customers
CSR	Ensuring that sources of supply, environmental impacts of product use and product disposal are increasingly considerate of the future well-being of all life on the planet

The primary challenge in any complex supply chain is alignment; that is, maintaining the appropriate flow of products or services from suppliers to customers in the face of unanticipated disruptions, changes in product design or service capabilities, and constant shifts in demand. The key to creating alignment is the rapid processing of information. This is turn requires integrated information technology platforms that communicate across entities, the ability to gather critical information that is needed to support decisions (these are called "decision support systems") and organizational arrangements among supply chain partners that allow rapid and effective decisions to be made.

In the old days, supply chain alignment was accomplished through personal relationships. People would literally write, visit or get in touch with one another to negotiate changes in the timing, quantity, quality or price of goods being sent down the supply chain. Because the work depended largely on personal relationships, people in the roles responsible for supply chain integration became adept at influence. In fact, some of the earliest social science research on interpersonal influence was carried out by studying the techniques that supply chain integrators used to push, cajole, trade favors, entreat, or threaten their counterparts into taking action.

While it still ultimately comes down to people, much of the work of supply chain integration is done automatically today through digital information processing platforms that are capable of managing the complexity of modern global supply chain operations. Once such systems are installed, they must be constantly updated to reflect changes in products, customers, suppliers, distributors, and forecasts of demand. Keeping systems up to date is crucial, since many millions of dollars of lost sales or spoiled goods can result from the system lagging behind the speed of the market. People who integrate supply chain operations spend most of their time managing exceptions, issues, and projects that are intended to enhance products, services, or supply. All of this must be done while respecting the legal frameworks within which business is conducted in different countries around the globe, observing existing contracts, and managing costs effectively. A braid that allows parties to engage readily in trust-based interactions is therefore extremely advantageous.

Coach, the New York-based manufacturer of designer handbags, discovered this as they sought to make cost-saving improvements in their supply chain through a number of independent projects. Because each of the projects was led by different individuals but ultimately affected the same entities that made up the global supply chain, it quickly became apparent that the projects were causing disruption as they competed for time, attention and resources. Bringing the project leaders together seemed like a rational thing to do but that alone did not solve the problem, since all the projects were deemed to be equally important and together, they overwhelmed the capacity of supply chain partners to implement.

Coach's supply chain partners also served other customers and found it difficult to incorporate some of the changes Coach wanted into their operations while fulfilling other contracts. The vast geographic distances involved meant that many discussions were not face-to-face, so "decisions" and "agreements" meant different things to different people. When Coach New York thought they had a firm commitment, suppliers in China felt they had the right to take the commitment as a suggestion, to be implemented if it could be done without disrupting their ongoing operations and contracts with other customers. Coach had treated them as vendors, not partners, in the past; the pressure to reduce costs and respond to an increasing set of demands had weakened the trust between the parties.

Once it realized that the problem wasn't getting solved, Coach dedicated a senior manager to the task of creating a more workable approach to implementing supply chain improvements. This leader made personal visits to the suppliers to build trust and understanding and then used the perspectives gained from interactions to design a new approach to collaborative decision making. Over time, this approach was aided by greater transparency in decision making and allowing supply chain partners to have a seat at the table when plans were being made. As partners were integrated into the new supply chain management tools that Coach built, the digital backbone enabled more frequent, real time communication that allowed rapid adjustments to be made. Trust grew and the new braided organization enabled Coach to work more effectively with its partners in introducing needed change.

The properties that make supply chain braids unique are the following.

- Partners in supply chain operations are independent entities with their own interests which are sometimes at odds with the interests of other partners; therefore, parties may not always be committed to the success of a particular project.
- Supply chain braids must do more than strengthen ties to create more reliable order fulfillment. They must also seek constant operational improvements and adapt to information regarding future customer demands. Independent entities must therefore coordinate investments that require time and capital in improvements that involve some degree of risk.
- Compared to other types of braids, supply chain braids are particularly dependent upon real-time big data analytics. Designing, building and constantly maintaining the digital platforms that provide these analytics requires high levels of expertise that is currently in short supply.
- Rapidly evolving technologies such as radio-frequency identification (RFID) devices, smart shelves, and equipment sensors will drive faster supply chain changes, making supply chain braids more essential and pushing the humans who participate in them to develop skills at more rapid joint decision making, experimentation, and collaboration across boundaries.

Making supply chain braids work involves overcoming these challenges. Doing that starts with recognition on the part of supply chain leaders that these issues exist and will not simply fade away with time. Deliberate actions are required to "get out there" and engage internal staff and external partners in the work of creating effective relationships that underlie supply chain innovation. Digital platforms and external supply chain operators provide the infrastructure. People make the infrastructure work as it is intended to work. Here is a checklist to use in diagnosing the current state and some recommended actions to create braids and develop them to their full potential (see Figures 4.5 and 4.6).

☐	Is the supply chain performing as it needs to perform?	☐	Are people across the boundaries of the supply chain at all levels able to take action to adjust as necessary to situations as they evolve?
☐	Are the relationships with suppliers strong and productive partnerships characterized by influence in both directions and co-evolution of capabilities?	☐	Are you using data analytics to optimize your response to changes in demand?
☐	Are there multiple points of connection among internal supply chain employees, suppliers and customers?	☐	Are you taking action in a timely fashion to obsolete existing products and add new products as the market demands?
☐	Are your goals for supply chain performance and those of your suppliers and customers aligned?	☐	Are you diversifying the supplier base while maintaining strong core relationships with key partners in order to optimize supply chain configuration?
☐	Is the digital platform you use to operate the supply chain capable of providing the kind of real-time data that can be used to make instantaneous decisions that influence supply chain outcomes?	☐	Do leaders encourage their people to in the supply chain to optimize the braid, form relationships with customers and suppliers, champion innovation and provide them with recognition when they do?
☐	Is your supply chain adapting quickly enough to changing customer demands and opportunities provided by new inventory management technologies?		

Figure 4.5. A diagnostic checklist for supply chain braid optimization.

The process of optimizing braids begins with an assessment of the current situation against a future ideal state of supply chain operation. To become a Walmart or Airbus takes an investment of time and energy, which can be justified by a comparison of the costs and benefits of the way the supply chain operates today versus the way it could operate in the future. If internal supply chain experts are not familiar with alternative supply chain management options or knowledgeable about current and future supply chain enhancement technologies, external help is readily available from a number of sources.

If the assessment reveals that innovation in supply chain design and management practices is warranted, the first step is to decide whether to

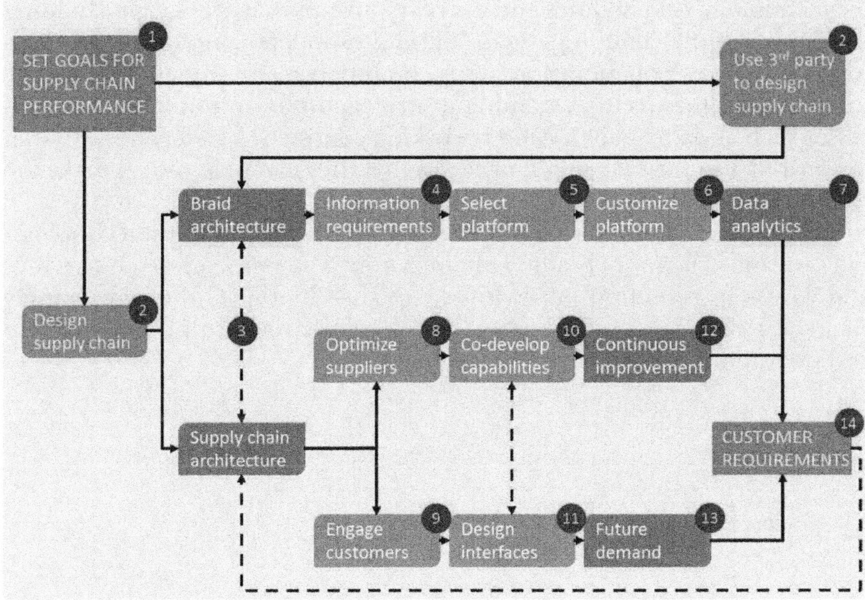

Figure 4.6. Optimizing supply chain braids.

turn the design over to a third party or do it yourself, as indicated in Figure 4.6. The pros and cons of this choice are obvious: greater speed to solution with external operators versus more control over key decisions through internal design.

The two elements of design are the technical backbone of the system and the organizational architecture to animate the braid. Excellent technical platforms exist on the market to manage even highly complex supply chain operations. Dassault 3DS, for example, is a system created by the French aircraft manufacturer based on its own experience in managing an extremely complex, time-sensitive supply chain that needed to perform perfectly or face severe consequences. Few organizations face this extreme level of challenge; it is a safe bet that if the system could handle Dassault's supply chain, it can probably handle yours.

Any system will need to be customized to work with the products, customer specifications, and information requirements of the supply chain in question. Further, to be useful, the system will need to be extended backward to suppliers of suppliers and forward to customers and product life cycle partners.

On the organizational side, talent, culture, work processes, roles, responsibilities, and leadership need to be realigned to support the way the braid is intended to operate. People need to develop the knowledge to exploit the technology's capabilities and the relationships that act like glue holding the entire supply chain together. Aligning suppliers, employees, and customers requires collaboration across boundaries, joint evolution of the supply chain architecture, training in new methods, introducing new processes such as data analytics and reworking contracts. Leaders need to step forward first in the learning journey so that they can help others make the right decisions along the way.

Supply chain braids are one of the fastest growing and most technologically advanced forms of braided organization. The tremendous cost savings and customer retention imperatives explain why this is the case. Supply chain braids are quickly becoming the gold standard of supply chain design and operation.

CHAPTER 5

IMPLEMENTING BRAIDS

Imagine that your organization had a project to accomplish that would be impossible if you were restricted to using your own resources. Certainly, that is the case for several of the organizations we have written about in this book, like Red Hat, Airbus, and Procter & Gamble. Here is another: *Golf Digest* magazine. The impossible project that *Golf Digest* must accomplish every 2 years is to rate the top 350 golf courses in the United States. Imagine the time and costs that would be involved in sending more than 10 *Golf Digest* staff members to play each of those courses. Would not happen. So how do they do it? Using a braid.

Golf Digest relies on a large group (currently 954) of excellent golfers (based on their official handicaps) who travel at their own expense to play and rate approximately two dozen courses each. Because *Golf Digest* is interested in assessing seven different characteristics of each course to determine its rating, they have recently decided to double the size of the rating group by 2020 in order to assure statistical accuracy. What is interesting to note is the language they used in their call to potential new members of the braid. Here are some excerpts from the letter written by the editor.

> Want to become a panelist? We'll tell you up front: It's a thankless but ultimately rewarding activity.... It's not cheap; panelists pay a membership fee and are expected to pay their own travel and lodging costs.... Every two years panelists get a letter grade on how they are doing.... Panelists are welcomed into a lot of great private courses, but if they accept so much as a

Braided Organizations: Designing Augmented Human-Centric Processes to Enhance Performance and Innovation, pp. 105–117

> lunch or logoed shirt, they'll be booted off the panel.... Golfers with young families are probably not going to have enough time to dedicate to course evaluations.... So do panelists get to play the exalted Top 10? Don't count on it.... The added benefit of the panel is the camaraderie that comes with kindred spirits who communicate via the panel's website and assist each other in getting on courses and reciprocating. (February, 2017).

It almost sounds like *Golf Digest* is trying to talk people out of joining the panel. In fact, they are communicating that the panel is an elite club and that only people who can afford the time and expense, are excellent golfers, and want to be able to brag to their friends about being on the panel and the courses that they get to play should sign up. They have succeeded in getting people to take on this work on a voluntary basis since 1966.

Perhaps the most frequent question we hear from leaders who are contemplating forming a braid is, "Why would anyone do this? Won't we have to pay them to get them to play?" As the *Golf Digest* example illustrates, people are willing to pay *Golf Digest* for the privilege of being on the rating panel. Not only does *Golf Digest* not pay people to join their braid, *it is actually a profit center*. The trick is to figure out what would make joining a braid attractive for people. In *Golf Digest's* case, it is what we mentioned earlier plus the ability to access courses through other members of the braid that they would normally not be allowed to play. Want to play Augusta National, home of the Masters? Someone on the panel is a member there and can get you on. That is worth a lot to people who care about the game of golf. For some, it's a life goal.

Not everyone is into golf. Some people are into coding software; others like developing apps. Some are dedicated to quality assurance and like spending time with others who share their passion. Some like the idea of belonging to an elite community of medical researchers seeking a cure to cancer. Some just like a chance to be creative which their day jobs do not allow. Getting a braid started is not as difficult as you might imagine, but making it successful takes some effort.

GETTING STARTED

We have discussed various kinds of braids and what it takes to make them work effectively. Hopefully, by now, you are thinking about where a braid could be useful to you or how to liven up the braids you already have. Of course, reading and thinking about braids will only get you so far; now it's time to take action. In this chapter, we describe the steps required to set up and operate braids. With the caution that every braid will have different twists and turns, Figure 5.1 provides a roadmap that you can follow.

Getting started involves learning about braids, understanding where they might add value and setting some specifications for what they are to achieve. This work begins at the strategic level and then is usually delegated to a team for detailed planning and execution.

Learn about braids and their applications. If you have read the previous chapters, you have a good head start on understanding where braids can be applied and how they can be successful. Although the inner workings of digital platforms are not something executives need to study, they do need to understand that implementing braids is a strategy that requires investment. To be committed to those investments, executives should be clear about the business case for braids they are about to create. Developing the business case is an iterative exercise. First, you learn about braids; then you think about how they could be applied; then you imagine the benefits that could accrue if they were successful; then you pilot a braid on a small scale to see if your assumptions are correct; then you revise your goals and expectations based on what is learned.

This approach may sound vaguely familiar to you. The chances are very good that you have observed or been affected directly by a decision to invest a huge amount of money in an information system that in the end did not live up to its promises. A question that few executives ask in these circumstances is, "How much of this was our fault because we didn't really understand what we were buying and what it would take to make it work?" The same outcomes will almost certainly result from the implementation of braids if leaders don't understand what is required of them and the organization to make braids work.

We have tried to be as clear as we can in previous chapters about what each type of braid needs to make it work. The issues are known. We advise strongly against braids being initiated at lower levels of authority than the support that is required to sustain them. The idea that, "We'll just build it and they will see how great it is" sounds attractive but does not work in practice because of the resources and agreements that are required to make braids work as well as they are intended. Leaders at the strategic level need to know what they are getting into and why.

Reading about braids is a place to start but seeing braids in action or even becoming a part of one is better. Descriptions of braids are like maps. They are accurate, but they do not really convey what a traveler will encounter along the way. Photos of New Zealand can provide a sense of its natural beauty but will never compare with being there in person. Even virtual reality goggles have not quite got it right yet; the temperature, the wind, the smells, the conversations, the food; these are the things that will keep people getting on airplanes instead of watching New Zealand from their couch (see Figure 5.1).

Time →

GETTING STARTED	DESGNING THE BRAID	TRIGGERING THE BRAID	OPERATING THE BRAID	TERMINATING THE BRAID
• Learn about braids and their application	• Study similar braids	• Internal staffing	• Participate actively	• Signal termination
• Consider opportunities to apply braids	• Select or create the digital platform	• Communications	• Shape conversations	• Share accomplishments
• Prioritize opportunities	• Design the architecture of the braid	• Targeted invitations	• Support informal leaders	• Preview coming attractions
• Set braid purpose and objectives	• Describe braid membership	• Engage external partners	• Continue to broaden ecosystem involvement	
• Set braid parameters	• Develop agreements regarding contractual work, IP		• Prioritize ecosystem relationships over time	
• Create the business case	• Create role descriptions for key positions in the braid		• Rapid prototyping of solutions	
• Designate braid design team	• Specify processes		• Publicize progress	

Figure 5.1. Inplementing braids.

To take part in a braid is an emotional experience. It is more than a chat online. To be a committed member of a community with a purpose, full of people with beautiful minds and senses of humor is moving, challenging, humbling, and thrilling. Reading about America's greatest golf courses is different than playing them.

The main reason for not investing in braids is not the cost. It is the belief that the same work could be accomplished by the people already on the payroll using the same approaches that have always been in place. Reading about braids will not dispel that notion. Only taking part in one will convince someone that this really is a different and better way to work.

Consider opportunities to apply braids. Senior leaders should have set a general direction but within that the braid team needs to investigate a range of purposes the braid or braids could fulfill. There are tradeoffs between the formality of the braid, the permanency of its membership, how open it is to guidance from external parties, whether it requires agreements with designated partners and more. What type and form of braid is appropriate will depend on the purposes the braid is intended to serve.

Even before the braid team begins investigating options, we recommend that the team agree on the criteria they will use to make their recommendation about which braids should be pursued. We find that this is one of the most important steps in the process, since agreeing on criteria at the beginning eliminates a great deal of conflict and rework later on.

Prioritize opportunities. The criteria developed by the team are used to assess each opportunity to form a braid in comparison to others. We recommend against starting multiple braids at once due to the investments of time, money and attention from senior leadership required. Once an organization has experience with designing and forming braids, additional braids are easier to get going. Starting with fewer and doing it right is a better strategy than the "natural selection" model of starting many and seeing which survive.

Set braid purpose and objectives. When initiating braids, it is tempting to forego setting specific objectives that a braid should accomplish. Due to the uncertainty, most braids will begin with vague hopes for making something better and no specific timeline for doing so. As with any project, lax goals produce a low sense of urgency. We know from research that optimal goals present challenges that are difficult but achievable. These kinds of goals elicit the highest level of energy and commitment. Not setting stretch goals for a braid seems reasonable at first but in actuality, may impede success. Individuals and teams need to have a real stake in the outcomes or the braid will be regarded as something to get around to when time allows—if ever.

Set braid parameters. Once goals are defined, the desired size, scope, and timeframe of a braid can be established. The size of the *Golf Digest* braid was determined by the need for statistical accuracy in the panel's rating of golf courses but also driven by a desire to generate additional revenue. The membership of the braid was carefully defined by a requirement that golfers provide evidence through their official handicaps that they are good players, and that the person is willing to evaluate approximately two dozen courses in a year's time. Golfers who joined the panel were allowed to stay for as long as they wished, providing they upheld the required ethics and performance standards. The Airbus supply chain braid was of a different nature. There, people from Airbus were assigned to the braid and vendors were asked to do the same, so that the individuals involved could begin to develop relationships and expertise over time that would allow improvements in how the supply chain was managed. In Eric Abouf's startup, the braid began with the owners of the company and a few investors and clients. As the organization grew, so did the braid. The objective of the next few steps is to ensure that the braid is designed for purpose.

Create the business case. The braid purpose and objectives explain what the braid should accomplish. The business case explains why this is important. We find that memory cannot be trusted; if a braid runs into difficulties initially, people seem to forget why it was important to install the braid in the first place. The business case doesn't have to be detailed but it does need to stand as a reminder of the commitment to see the braid through to success.

Designate a braid setup team. Top leaders need to understand why braids are important, a little bit about how they work and where they could be applied. Once this is accomplished, those leaders need to empower a team to start working on the details of exactly what type of braid is needed and how it will operate.

This team needs a good mixture of perspectives, from some people who understand digital platforms to others who know how the business operates and others who understand customers or partners. Six to seven people should be the maximum size of the team to keep things moving. They should be people who are trusted by senior leaders but are probably not senior leaders themselves unless the braid is an entrepreneurial braid in a startup company. Others, including people outside the organization can be added to the team temporarily from time to time. The work of the internal braid team is likely to require full-time attention for a week to several months, followed by anything from permanent full-time assignments to a few hours a week depending on the nature of the braid. At least a few of the members of the team should be passionately committed to working in the braid and staying with it through its lifecycle.

Study similar braids. Once the general nature of the braid is decided (entrepreneurial, open innovation, organizational integration, supply chain management, and so forth) it makes sense to learn from others who have cut trails in the new territory that you wish to explore. As the philosopher Friedrich Nietzche (1996) said, "When one has finished building one's house, one suddenly realizes that in the process one has learned something that one really needed to know in the worst way—before one began." Learning from others can help to avoid the kinds of unpleasant surprises to which Nietzche is referring.

Select or create the digital platform. While small braids can operate without a digital platform other than email, most braids will require a platform that is specifically designed to support the work of the braid as the braid grows. While some platforms like Slack or Dassault Systemes' 3DS are available "off the shelf" there will undoubtedly be some customization required. In less formal braids, an off-the-shelf platform will represent a minimal expense. In complex supply chain braids the digital backbone is an essential tool requiring a great deal of customization and an expensive one to be certain.

Design the architecture of the braid. Here we get to the part of designing the braid that is like determining the way the plumbing, electrical and heating systems will work in a house. As we saw in chapter two, the digital braid must provide a reliable means of communication across internal and external boundaries, involving the right people who have access to the right conversations and information. Braids may also access databases that provide the common knowledge that members need to make coordinated but independent adjustments to achieve joint activities. Communities of practice will require their own chat rooms so that they do not have to wade through irrelevant clutter to get to messages that matter. Data feeds from sensors in field locations need to send data at the right time to the right place, and that data needs to be analyzed to provide useful information.

Anyone who has been involved in an exercise to understand why sales dropped ten percent in the last month will recognize how difficult it is to isolate the variables that could have caused the anomaly. Without access to the right information, hypotheses can't be tested. If the data were never collected in the first place, accurate explanations are impossible to manufacture. Organizations get better over time in such matters because they learn from experience that they do not know what they need to know. It is an example of the kind of knowledge that Nietzche was speaking about.

Braid designers can't expect to get everything right in advance. One of the most amazing benefits of braids is that they learn and become smarter over time. Still, the time taken to anticipate the needs of members and leaders will save frustrating delays or mistakes later on.

Describe braid membership. *Golf Digest* has a very clear idea of who the members of their braid should be. Having the wrong people join your braid and empowering them to influence key decisions is like having the passengers fly the plane. You want qualified pilots up front, not people who have no idea what they are doing. To large extent, braids are self-policing, in that smart members know what smart members sound like. They can quickly detect if a person is clueless regarding the topic at hand and can say so out loud, because members are not beholden to one another, may never know one another personally, or work together again. Still, only good can come from stating the qualities of individuals who are welcome in the braid and the behaviors members are expected to exhibit. Reducing the frustration of dealing with bad members will help sustain the energy and commitment of good members.

Develop agreements regarding contractual work, IP. Potential members who are not employees of the host organization in open innovation braids and entrepreneurial braids will seek clarity about their interests in intellectual property or ownership. Some open innovation braid host organizations contract specifically with members of the braid who offer promising solutions to the challenges they wish to solve. Entrepreneurial braid members may be offering financial support or other services in exchange for a percentage of shares or profits. Braids have different logics regarding the interests of external parties. There are no right or wrong answers but clarity among all parties is important to prevent legal issues from arising.

Create role descriptions for key positions in the braid. More complex braids need people to assume roles for directing traffic, providing projects for the braid to work on, analyzing data feeds so that decisions can be made, ensuring follow through on commitments, enforcing agreements, and recruiting the right members to join. Supply chain braids, for example, need points of contact within each partner organization who can direct resources to respond to the coordination inputs they receive through the braid. Hosts of open innovation braids need people who will evaluate the ideas that are provided by external parties.

Research on "gatekeepers," people who provide access to knowledge or resources in research and development organizations has shown that people should not be appointed to the gatekeeper role against their wishes. When that happens, they perform much less effectively than people who have are passionate about the role and have a natural inclination to do the things that the role requires: keeping up with the literature, sharing knowledge that others might find useful, connecting people to others with shared interests, and spending time working on challenges that others are facing. Therefore, when appointing people to roles in a braid, it is important to make sure they are right for the job.

Specify processes. While Wikipedia is based on open source contributions, there is an established process people to become authorized to make additions or updates. Proposed changes are not made without being reviewed by an expert group. At Procter & Gamble, the open source innovators don't award their own contracts; people at P&G decide that. At Airbus, when engineers make changes to aircraft designs that require vendors to change their manufacturing processes, every detail must be recorded and authorized by the proper aviation authorities. Braids are not the Wild West; while a great deal of what happens is informal and led by the community, when decisions are made that affect quality, spending or safety, decisions processes need to be in place so that everyone involved understands how the braid works and what is required of them.

TRIGGERING THE BRAID

Once the braid is designed, it is time to fire up the engine and see how it performs. Like the operation of the braid, its inception is more organic than tightly managed.

Internal staffing. Braids need tending. A core group of people, ranging from a few to up to as many as 50 need to devote time to triggering the braid, monitoring its work, and recommending actions that should be taken based on the outputs produced. This team, like the braid design team, needs to understand both the work of the braid and the technology behind the digital backbone. As a team, they need to be tightly aligned on the purpose of the braid and buy into the objectives for its performance. The time spent by various team members will differ depending on their responsibilities but there absolutely must be a commitment on their part to attend regular meetings where the performance of the braid is reviewed and additional actions to support the braid are considered. An executive may call meetings of the team but like the braid itself, meetings are most effective if they are facilitated by members of the team, who should also make decisions about what they need to do.

Communications. Getting the braid up and running requires a variety of communication methods and continued efforts over time. In the beginning, the core team needs to define and communicate the purpose of the braid to potential members. Since the attractiveness of the invitation is critical, engaging a close-in group of likely members in reviewing and rewriting the statement of purpose is helpful. The core team should identify a list of people they would most like to have participate in the braid. These people should be brought together physically or virtually to form the nucleus of the first-generation braid. If they sign on, they should use their contacts to expand the membership to create the second-generation braid, and so on until the braid develops the characteristics sought after in the design phase. Often, in the initial stages of the braid, personal conversations are necessary to convince parties that their participation would be worthwhile. In some braids, these conversations will extend to include formal contracts or conditions of membership.

Like everything else in braids, growing the membership is an iterative, trial and error process. Some parties are a natural fit and others struggle to find the relevance of the braid to them or the time they need to get involved. The goal should not be to retain one hundred percent of those who are recruited but instead to reach the point where the braid is highly functioning with a committed membership as quickly as possible.

Targeted invitations. Just as in the formation of the braid, targeted invitations to individuals or parties can be extended as the work progresses and the need for specialized knowledge or connections becomes apparent. Unless braids remain open to new members, discussions may become centered around a few ideas or individuals. The key function of a braid is either coordination or solution creation. If key parties with vital links or specialized knowledge are missing, the braid will perform at a lower level than desired. To keep the braid fresh and optimize its effectiveness, members may be queried to suggest the names of others who could fill important gaps and those parties can be invited personally to join. Core team members can bring these parties quickly up to speed so that their initial contributions add immediate value to the conversations.

Engage external partners. Core members also carry responsibility for establishing connections with partners who are essential to the work of the braid. In supply chain braids, for example, getting vendors to join the braid, participate, install necessary data systems and take appropriate actions in a timely fashion is necessary of the braid is to perform its function. As we discussed in the supply chain chapter, vendors may have multiple customers, so getting them to pay attention to the requirements of the host braid can be a challenge. The right incentives must be in place to make the partnership attractive. Members of the core team who interface with various vendors also need to be able to influence the host organization to adapt to partners' needs.

OPERATING THE BRAID

Braids will naturally experience ebbs and flows in energy over time. The core team can take certain actions that maintain a higher level of energy than otherwise would be the case.

Participate actively. Members of the core team should actively participate in the braid. Only a few people are required to keep conversations flowing. Given that the purpose of the braid is to access knowledge or shape the behavior of parties outside the core, active participation by core members should be aimed primarily at encouraging that participation.

The core team should avoid taking over or simply having conversations with one another. As they get to know the key influencers through their contributions, core team members should make contributions that magnify and accelerate the contributions of key parties.

Shape conversations. Core team members, through their active participation, can remind people in the braid of the purpose they are trying to achieve when conversations start to go in directions that are counterproductive. Members have a wide range of interests and personal agendas that are not always conducive to the braid. If other members of the braid do not comment on this, core members will need to do so.

Support informal leaders. Core members should act as cheerleaders in recognizing good inputs from informal leaders of the braid. By the judicious use of positive reinforcement, core members can signal to others what is expected. Recognition is one of the most important rewards that individuals receive in return for their contributions to the braid.

Continue to broaden ecosystem involvement. As mentioned previously, bringing in new parties with fresh perspectives can help maintain the interest level within the braid. As the braid grows, it becomes more attractive to potential members. If new members happen to be highly respected individuals within the community, so much the better. As the braid becomes recognized as a place where elite parties gather, it will pick up momentum and make recruitment that much easier. At some point however, it's desirable to begin restricting membership in the braid and to make entry more difficult.

Prioritize ecosystem relationships over time. With experience, you will come to recognize that some partners are better contributors, more reliable, or easier to work with than others. The goal is not to create the largest braid possible but the highest performing one. Size brings complexity and slows things down; once you have a critical mass of good contributors and you are making progress toward your goal, you can narrow the braid to those few, adding others only when necessary.

Rapid prototyping of solutions. Braids thrive on making progress toward objectives or solutions. Undertaking many small experiments provides a continuous stream of reinforcement, whether the experiments are successes or failures. The important thing is that members of the braid experience that they are getting somewhere, not simply engaging in interesting conversations.

Publicize progress. Because progress is important in sustaining the motivation of members, the core team should try different ways of sharing the braid's achievements. Varying the way this news is disseminated helps keep it interesting, making it more effective in maintaining motivation. Some braids have annual award ceremonies that recognize individuals for their contributions. Progress should be publicized in the host organization, since the continued support of leadership is essential to maintain the operation of the braid and encourage investments in its recommendations.

TERMINATING THE BRAID

Some braids are intended to have a short life. A specific problem can be solved, or challenge met. If that is the case, the way the braid is terminated can affect how easy it is to reengage members of the braid if they are needed in the future.

Signal termination. The most important action in terminating a braid is simply to make it clear that the braid has met its purpose and is being disbanded. Although this seems obvious, host organizations that are excited to find a solution to a vexing problem sometimes forget to let members of the braid know that they have reached the finish line.

Share accomplishments. Members may not realize exactly what the braid has accomplished. Making this clear reinforces the shared feeling of success and enhances the attractiveness of the community should it be asked to take on another challenge down the road.

Preview coming attractions. If plans are in the works for the formation of additional braids, let people know so that they can reserve time in their schedules to participate if their expertise is needed. Parties are more likely to join a braid with people they know and like than to join an entirely new community.

IMPLICATIONS FOR CEOs, EXECUTIVE TEAMS, AND BOARDS

The implications of adopting braids for CEOs, Executive Teams, and Boards are both strategic and operational. Decisions about when to form braids and how much to invest in them are clearly strategic. There are no right or wrong answers, but these decisions definitely matter. Once braids are formed, they do not perform if left on autopilot with little or no attention from the leadership of the host organization. Knowing the operational ins and outs of braids and providing appropriate oversight is as important to the success of braids as it is to the impact of programs like Six Sigma.

For CEOs, the main issue to be aware of is that traditional organizations will likely resist forming braids, meaning that strong leadership from the CEO will be required to move ahead. Imagine that you were in the research and development organization at Procter & Gamble before A.G. Lafley led the organization into open innovation. Your stance would likely be, "let us try this on our own first; if we can't do it, then we can let others try." P&G had and still has a marvelous research organization, staffed with brilliant scientists and an admirable track record. Imagine the discomfort people experienced with Lafley's insistence that unknown outsiders should be involved. Without his leadership, it's doubtful that P&G would be where it is today in terms of open innovation.

Of course, triggering a braid is the first act of strategic importance. Making certain that the right talent is assigned to operating a braid and that investments are made in the digital backbone and solutions generated by a braid will also require CEO support.

Individual executive team members may be involved in initiating a braid. Regardless of the interest of individual members of the team, the team as a whole must align regarding the requirements for operating a successful braid. Working across silos is always a challenge. Politics within the executive team make the challenge that much greater. Braids will not work if the responsibility for the braid is delegated to an individual executive who is thereafter not supported by his or her peers.

This means that all members of the executive team need to understand how braids work and what the implications of that understanding are for how their units or departments need to operate differently to support the braid. If we return to the P&G example, while the head of research and development might have primary responsibility for the open innovation braid, everyone around the table has an important role to play. Manufacturing needs to be prepared to implement changes that will allow breakthrough products to be made; marketing will need to support not just advertising but shifts in the breadth of the brand; legal will have to devote time to understanding the organization's stance toward intellectual capital and preparing contracts with external parties; and human resources will address issues around employment, compensation and organization design. Procter & Gamble operates differently today than it did in the pre-open innovation era. Many changes have been made which were not foreseen and learning needed to take place over time. The point is that braids will not reach their potential if members of the executive team believe that making the braid successful is not their collective responsibility. Executive team members also need to understand the leadership requirements of braids and how they differ from what traditional leaders may be doing. Executive team members shape the culture of the organization and set expectations for how others lead.

Boards of directors should play a proactive role in questioning whether braids are being considered for purposes where they could add value. Bringing an external perspective, boards are well-positioned to help formulate braid strategies and also comment on how well braids are being operated. To do this, boards need to learn about braids. If they lack personal experience with braids, board members may choose to use their connections to visit other organizations where braids are in use to learn from those with first-hand knowledge.

CHAPTER 6

LEADING BRAIDS

We met Jim Whitehurst, the CEO of the Linux open-source company Red Hat in Chapter 4. Having spent his career in traditional organizations prior to joining Red Hat, Whitehurst (2015) writes that the adjustment to the world of Red Hat was full of mistakes and learning for him.

> Top-down decision making simply doesn't work in a company like Red Hat whose business model depends on collaboration and shared ideas, rather than control of assets.... Our people expect—actually they demand—to have a voice in how we run the company, ranging from the mission statement to the travel policy. As CEO, I can't simply send orders down the ranks and expect everyone to jump on board. In order to drive engagement and collaboration to the roots of an organization, you need to get people involved in the decision-making process. And you know what? It works. Red Hat is a faster, leaner, and more innovative company as a result.

So, if command and control is out in braided companies where many of the most important contributors aren't even on the payroll, what do leaders of braided companies do? Are they totally irrelevant or even worse, a drag on innovation? Actually, the answer is "no." Even though Whitehurst leads differently now than in the past, he is still earning his pay.

Braids, like organizations, have both formal and informal leaders. Both are essential to the success of a braid. As shown in Figure 6.1, formal leaders provide the purpose and resources for the braid while informal leaders

Braided Organizations: Designing Augmented Human-Centric Processes to Enhance Performance and Innovation, pp. 119–131

help to direct energy, knowledge identification and solution development within the braid.

FORMAL LEADERSHIP

- Defines the initial purpose and objectives of the braid
- Determines who should staff different roles in the braid in order to launch it
- Provides resources to create the digital platform the braid will use to operate
- Aligns the organization structure, culture and work processes with the braid
- Decides whether to sanction the solutions created by the braid
- Determines when the braid should cease operation

INFORMAL LEADERS

- Provide energy, expertise and initiate connections with others
- Help figure out the best way to approach the work
- Guide the development of proposed solutions
- Help set the tone and level of commitment within the braid
- Provide unsolicited feedback
- Call for changes in direction, braid composition or braid operation as needed
- Coalesce decisions

Figure 6.1. Formal and informal leadership in braids.

First, let us address the work of formal leaders. Leaders define the initial purpose of the braid and its objectives. If the purpose or objectives are unattractive, others who are essential to the performance of the braid will not join or will not stay. Parties in the braid contribute voluntarily because they are inspired by the purpose, see benefits to themselves by doing so and find the rewards and contributions balanced. There are no command performances except by members of the host organization itself, and even they are unlikely to do what is required to make the braid succeed if they are in disagreement with its purpose.

Leaders need to staff the braid with people who will trigger it. For braids involving external parties, this activity may involve a general "call to arms" to see who responds, or it may involve a series of meetings with supply chain partners. The requirements for staffing will depend on the type of braid and the help needed.

Next, like any other IT effort, leaders decide the scope of investments in braid platforms. Parties who join the braid won't make these investments, so formal leaders who expect to benefit from the braid must provide funding and oversight.

Another job for leaders is to shift the organization structure and culture to support the work of braids. Simply laying technology over a siloed, hierarchical organization with cumbersome processes will not fix the problems that braids might address. Poor relationships with external partners, such as vendors or customers, will not be resolved simply by inviting them to join a braid. Fixing the underlying problems that will interfere with the performance of the braid is still a job for formal leadership. Members of a braid can work around barriers but only to a point. Eventually, if the barriers are not removed, they will take their ideas and energy elsewhere.

As the braids produce ideas for action, someone needs to make the decision as the whether the recommendations should be followed. Often, acting on the recommendations entails costs and risks of various kinds, both large and small. Since a braid is not a legal entity, it does not possess a bank account and can't receive venture funding. That's something that formal leaders must provide.

Finally, if the purpose of the braid is fulfilled it may make sense to terminate the braid and begin a new one. Some braids are perpetual, meaning that their purpose is ongoing. These braids will continue as long as the host organization exists and supports them. Other braids are intended to be short-lived, such as braids that are created to achieve a particular breakthrough via open innovation. If the braid is temporary, formal leaders will make the decision that it is time to close the braid down.

These functions performed by formal leaders are absolutely critical to the initiation and optimization of the braid's performance. Whether they are performed by leaders of an organization or by a core group of founders of the braid (think Wikipedia), these actions create the vessel within which a braid can operate.

At the same time, *informal leaders* play even more important roles in braided organizations than in traditional organizations. Informal leaders bring the braid to life in the following ways.

Informal leaders provide energy, expertise, and connections. If you have attended a good party lately, you may remember the food or music. However, it is more likely that you will remember the people who made the event special. The same is true for braids. Who shows up and what they do matters. Informal members who bring energy, expertise, and expand the circle of connections are the true superstars when it comes to how well a braid performs. Their energy makes the braid attractive to others, increasing membership and prolonging interactions within the braid. The role these informal leaders play is especially important as the work of the braid encounters challenges. If informal leaders take the challenges in stride or even better, find them energizing, others will as well.

Informal leaders also help to figure out how to get the work done. In most braids, the nature of the work involves uncertainty. Answers are not always known, and neither is the way to find them. As a collection of independent or loosely connected individuals, braids could flounder, and members become frustrated if it was not for the voices of informal leaders coalescing around an approach to explore, even if only for a short time until more is known. Braids work best when their energy is focused and directed, albeit by consensus rather than dictate.

The same applies to developing final recommendations or solutions. There is an infinite number of things that could be tried but only the resources and willingness to try a few. Deciding which solutions provide the best chance of working is not an easy thing for a large, virtual community to do. Voting is possible, and the wisdom of the crowd is certainly valuable. Still, informal leaders who are experts may see flaws that others do not. The process of working toward a chosen solution is one that must be managed delicately. A heavy hand by a few will drive away others whose expertise is sorely needed. Banter, humor, debates and last calls for divergent thinking are tools in the kit of good informal braid leaders.

Effective braids survive on a diet of serious intent and playful interaction. Braids that are run like a military operation soon find themselves without members. Braids that are constant fun without making meaningful progress produce nothing of value, even if people enjoy belonging to them. The "fun" that is needed is the experience of success; the back-slapping, high-fiving thrill that comes from doing something really difficult that has never been done before or done as well. Informal leaders know when to move from pure brainstorming to the harder work of narrowing down the alternatives without taking the enjoyment out of the process. People in braids thrive on recognition and informal leaders know how to dispense it artfully. People join braids that "feel right" not just because they present interesting challenges but because they sense that they will enjoy the work with others.

Informal leaders need to know when to call it as they see it. If the host organization's purpose for the braid is uninspiring, they need to say so and suggest an alternative. If the incentives being offered for open innovation ideas are too small to make participating in the braid worthwhile, someone needs to wave that flag. Formal leaders need to know what's going on in the braid that could kill it or impair its progress. Informal leaders who see things from an objective perspective, having nothing to lose and are in touch with the vibe of the braid are in the best position to do that.

The most critical unsolicited feedback informal leaders can provide is to say that the braid simply isn't working and never will, unless something about it is changed. If a braid is stalling out but another pathway may provide opportunities, informal leaders need to start moving people in that new direction. Just as excitement builds gradually during the inception of a braid, informal leaders need to start gradually building excitement about replacing the old purpose with a new one. If the hosts of the braid disagree with the new direction, they can pull the plug and the braid will die. Before doing so, hosts need to weigh the possibility that the informal leaders could be right.

The work of braids is open-ended, ongoing, and iterative, meaning that it is difficult to decide when the braid has reached a point where a particular effort at innovation or improvement has achieved victory. Further improvement is always possible. At some point, in order to reap the benefit of the work done, informal leaders need to declare success and help coalesce agreement to implement a solution. A new round of innovation can begin after the solution is implemented.

In these ways, formal and informal leaders work in complementary fashions to optimize the performance of braids. Neither friendly chats on Facebook nor command and control organization of activities is the goal with braids. Braids are purposeful, nonhierarchical, living organisms made up of people and entities that want to get something done because they are committed rather than required to do so. Formal leaders make the work possible but informal leaders make the work happen.

WHAT FORMAL LEADERS NEED TO KNOW ABOUT LEADING IN BRAIDS

The most important thing for leaders to know is that leading in a braided organization is not like leading in a traditional hierarchical organization. As Jim Whitehurst learned from his experience, leaders of braided organizations should expect their authority to be questioned. Respect in a braid is earned and authority is granted, not imposed. It takes a person with an open mind and visionary drive to lead a braid effectively. Table 6.1 contrasts traditional and braid leadership.

Power. In a traditional organization, "rank has its privileges." The higher the rank, the more the power, in theory. In braided organizations, it's what a person contributes that matters. Whitehurst (2015) explains, "At Red Hat, some of the seven thousand voices inside the company have far more sway than others. In most cases, decisions aren't made by consensus. Rather, those people who have earned their peers' respect over time drive decisions." That's *anyone* who has earned their peers' respect; not just

Table 6.1.
Traditional Versus Braid Leadership

LEADERSHIP DIMENSIONS	TRADITIONAL LEADERSHIP		BRAID LEADERSHIP
POWER	Positional	>	Value of contributions
ORGANIZATION LOGIC	Top-down, bounded	>	Bottom-up, unbounded
STYLE	Command and control	>	Commitment
PSYCHOLOGICAL CONTRACT	Mandatory compliance	>	Voluntary cooperation
STANCE	Suspicion	>	Trust
REWARDS	Financial	>	Psychological
CONTROLS	Rules	>	Processes
DIVERSITY	Threat	>	Asset
EMOTIONS	Distracting	>	Essential
RESPONSE TO ISSUES	Take control	>	Ask for help
ORIENTATION	Drive results	>	Create possibilities
TEAMWORK	Optional, wasteful	>	Fundamental, efficient
DECISION MAKING	Logical, fact-based	>	Iterative, intuitive
DISRUPTION	Negative	>	Positive

people with titles. The people with the greatest influence in a braided organization may not even work for the company; they may be nonpaid thought leaders who have made contributions that are clearly valuable. In the Red Hat braid, as in other open innovation braids in the software world, “Code talks.” What this means is that good programming is recognized by other expert programmers. There is a common measuring stick by which people make decisions about who should be paid attention to.

Of course, as the “Chief initiator” of the braid, Whitehurst does have formal influence, but not the kind that some other CEOs rely upon. Here is how he describes his role,

> My job is not about conjuring up brilliant strategies and making people work harder. What I need to do is create the context for Red Hat associates so that they can do their best work. My goal is to get people to believe in the mission and then create the right structures that empower them to achieve what once might have been impossible.

Organization logic. What is the logic underlying how traditional organizations are designed and operate? If you are a leader with one hundred percent clarity about the work that needs to be done and your primary concern is getting people to do what you need them to do, *maybe* the Egyptian pharos had it right. Subjugate some people, threaten them with punishment if they do not do what you need them to do, and make an example of those who don't so that others get the message. Modern leaders are much more sophisticated and sensitive than that, of course, but the underlying logic remains the same—force people by whatever means—rewards for doing the job, punishment for not—to do work that they otherwise would not do. Have someone watch over them constantly so that they follow instructions, do not goof off, or steal from the company. We are being extremely harsh here to make a point. Putting a nicer face on reality by dressing it up with recognition, good benefits, or restricted involvement in goal-setting (meaning that people have some choice in setting their goals but not really that much) does not change the fundamental logic. The logic is still "we have work we need you to do; we will tell you what how and when; as long as you comply, we're open to hearing your suggestions about how we can do things better and may even be willing to let you join our team."

If leaders need to rely on associates and even people who do not work for the company to use their expertise to figure out what needs to be done and how, a different logic is required. It cannot be, "We know what needs to be done and all we need from you is to do it." It has to be, "We need your help. We can't get anywhere without you. We're interested in a partnership. We would like access to your expertise in exchange for something you value, whether it be compensation, recognition, a chance to work on an interesting challenge, be part of a community from which you can learn and develop —whatever it is, we'll do our best to make it happen. We're not going to tell you how to do your job because we wouldn't begin to know how. You'll need to help us understand the ways in which you can best contribute." This kind of organization logic shifts the locus of control from top-down to bottom-up. The focal organization sets the mission and provides the context, the tools, and the steady support for progress; the braid defines the best way to approach the work. If people make mistakes, everyone learns from them; no one is fired, although they may lose credibility with their peers over time. The focal organization still has the right to say no to the solutions developed, but their people can't jump in and take over if they do not like the direction the braid is taking. The braid holds the ultimate keys to progress.

Psychological contract. It follows that the implicit contract between members of the braid and the focal organization or mission of the braid is based on voluntary contribution. Braid members play as long as they feel there is benefit and fairness. In a traditional organization, the psychological contract goes something like this, "If you accept our terms of employment, we own you. We are allowed to tell you what to do and when to do it. We will also own your ideas and expect your complete loyalty. Any violation of these conditions will result in your immediate termination." Again, we are using extreme contrast to make the point. There is a good deal of research that addresses why people working under traditional psychological contracts choose to give voluntary effort to their organizations. Some people give much more than we might expect and this is called "organizational citizenship behavior" (Smith, Organ, & Near, 1983). They are like people who clean up the neighborhood or serve on the school board even though it is not their job. The majority of findings for why people go above and beyond is that it is either intrinsic to their values or they feel that their efforts will somehow be recognized if they just keep trying. So even in traditional organizations, some voluntary contributions take place. Of course, the opposite is also true; there is a percentage of people in traditional organizations who don't hold up their end of the bargain, even to the point of fulfilling their obligations. In braided organizations, these people simply drop out.

Employers are very concerned these days about engagement, because engaged employees contribute more and make customers happier than disengaged employees. If there are ways to get employees to give more for the same pay, why not engage them? In braided organizations, people are engaged, or they do not join or do not stay. If the positive effects of engagement are felt in traditional organizations when only a small percentage of people are truly engaged, imagine what it feels like to be part of an organization where *everyone* is engaged. The energy and creativity is amazing.

Stance. In traditional organizations, power is held tightly at the top and there is very little transparency about what is happening. This is because leaders have an inherent mistrust of their employees. Traditional leaders fear that employees might leak information, abscond with intellectual property, complain about decisions or in other ways make life difficult. In fact, these are things that people do when they feel oppressed, so leaders are right to be nervous. The history of sabotage is a long and interesting one (Dubois, 1979).

In braids, there is no reason to withhold information or mistrust members because members are the ones with the knowledge and expertise critical to success of the mission. While it is certainly a possibility that members of the braid will apply knowledge they gain to future endeavors, the knowledge would not exist in the first place without them. Host organizations win by supporting the creation of knowledge and exploiting it more effectively than others, not by withholding information or penalizing people for self-interests. There are exceptions to this. In open innovation efforts, for example, host organizations can contract to pay contributors to do research for the host organization which is retained as the property of the host and may not be applied elsewhere. Some host organizations have been known to sell the intellectual capital to the contractor if the host organization decides not to capitalize on what has been developed. Both parties benefit in the long-run from sharing knowledge and engaging in transparent communications.

Rewards. Leaders of traditional organizations rely primarily on financial rewards to secure initial commitment to join, engender loyalty over time, and incent effort. People in braids may or may not be compensated. In some braids, people join purely out of interest and stay only as long as they find their involvement psychologically rewarding. Therefore, the work of leaders in traditional organizations and braided organizations is different. Leaders in traditional organizations offer employment in exchange for compliance. In braided organizations, members figure out their own reasons for belonging to the braid. Leaders do not instruct, they support the braid by doing what they can to provide what the braid needs in exchange for the value the braid provides. It is as if the braid is the employer and leaders in the host organization work for the braid. While this may sound odd, remember how Jim Whitehurst described his role as CEO of Red Hat earlier in this chapter.

Controls. In traditional organizations, rules are created by those in authority and enforced by leaders. In braided organizations, rules may not even exist.

The thought an organization operating without rules is frightening to leaders who are used to working in a controlled culture. Having seen infractions of the rules, leaders may have trouble imagining what would occur if people were allowed to police themselves.

To use a sports analogy, it is a little bit like the contrast between football and golf. In football, referees are given the authority to call penalties because players would not call penalties on themselves and arguments between players and teams would never be settled. In golf, players are expected to call penalties on themselves; it is a matter of integrity.

As noted, the logics of traditional organizations and braided organizations are different, and this carries over to the issue of control. The logic of traditional organizations is a script to be followed, from which deviations are not acceptable. The logic of braided organizations is collaboration in service of a shared purpose. As long as a braid is working as intended, its members want it to operate successfully and are willing to do their part to make it so, including self-policing to the extent that it is required. Peers point out when a member is doing something they shouldn't do, such as monopolizing chats, failing to support open brainstorming, or not sharing knowledge or ideas. Peers cannot "fire" members of the braid but they can call attention to these kinds of behaviors and the braid community can then exert further pressure to bring parties into line.

Diversity. One of the great assets of braids is that demographic diversity is not a factor in who is allowed to influence ideas. Like orchestras that use blind auditions by having applicants play behind a screen so that biases regarding appearance do not cloud judgments about a person's abilities, braids allow people of any age, color, nationality, or background to be heard on an equal footing. Diversity in thinking is welcomed in braids because it makes for a richer and more fertile environment for learning and the development of solutions.

Emotions. Research by Jane McGonigal of the Institute for the Future reveals that people playing video games are much more engaged at an emotional level than most people are at work (McGonigal, 2011). In part, this is because in traditional organizations, emotions are viewed as distracting rather than essential to achieving results. Emotions in traditional organizations are considered dangerous if they involve negativity or unnecessary if they are positive. Better to simply keep one's head down and do the work.

Braided organizations run on emotion. Like being engaged in playing a video game, participating in a braid should feel exciting and inherently rewarding or people will not play. Breakthrough ideas are less likely to be discovered by people trudging along day after day, disengaged emotionally and simply keeping their heads down. Braids need spirited interactions to being them to life. As noted by Jim Whitehurst (2015), this even includes strong arguments that people who are used to working in traditional organizations would find a bit scary,

> Many see a highly collaborative culture as a supportive, positive environment where people encourage each other with positive reinforcement. Actually, Red Hat is anything but that. It is very supportive and collaborative, but in a different way. We debate, we argue, and we complain. In many ways, it can seem harsh. But iron sharpens iron, and we've come to embrace the notion of letting sparks fly.

Response to issues. Leaders in traditional organizations sometimes feel it is their job to dive into problems or challenges that are encountered. Once, when working with a manufacturing plant, we noticed that every time there was a problem with equipment in the assembly area, the plant manager would personally rush out to the floor, roll up his sleeves, and start working to repair the equipment. People he paid to perform this work stepped aside as he jumped in because he had made it clear to everyone that no one was as capable as he in diagnosing and repairing a problem. He had no awareness of the negative, disempowering impact his behavior was having on the organization. His ego was getting in the way of bright people contributing to solving a whole range of issues, whether they be mechanical or strategic. Today, we see boards and executive teams doing the same thing. The knee-jerk reaction to dive into the weeds and take over is almost irresistible.

Because braids run on the ideas and energy of their members, formal leaders cannot jump in and take over when there are issues, or the braid will lose its appeal to members. Braid members pride themselves on their problem-solving abilities and taking on challenges is part of what makes participation in the braid fun and worthwhile. When formal leaders determine that there is a problem or challenge that needs to be addressed by the braid, rather than taking over they need to ask for help. Like crowdsourcing, the response of the braid to the challenge is likely to be swift and effective.

Orientation. Leaders in traditional organizations drive results. They coax, exhort, demand action, and pound on the table to get attention. If results do not improve, the next level of intervention is to replace people in critical roles either because they lack the ability to produce results or simply to make a visible example to others of what happens when leaders are unsuccessful in meeting expectations.

Formal leaders can make the urgency of finding solutions clear as they set the purpose for braids and trigger their formation. Once the braid forms however their ability to control the pace of work is limited. Different kinds of braids and different size braids will work at different speeds. Leaders should consider this as they design and trigger braids. The tradeoff, obviously, is more knowledge availability in larger, less-structured braids versus a longer time for the braid to form and figure out how to work on solutions.

Teamwork. In traditional organizations, teamwork is possible in short bursts but generally resisted since it is difficult, time-consuming and not always productive. The preferred method for getting something done quickly is to assign someone to be in charge, give them the people and resources they need, and execute a plan to make it happen. That can work if the people assembled have the knowledge needed and know how to use it to create and execute the solution.

Braids are formed when internal knowledge is lacking or doing the work requires collaboration with people outside the organization. Braids are therefore dependent on teamwork. Assigning work to individuals would defeat the purpose of forming the braid in the first place. Instead of assigning responsibilities, informal leaders in braids take initiative where they can and invite others to join in where help is needed. Informal leaders also coalesce the work of others, so that the combined effort of parties in the braid are productive.

As technologies that are designed to support virtual teamwork continue to improve, work in braids can be almost as productive as bringing people together in a room. What makes braided teamwork better than face to face teamwork is that you could never fit everyone in a braid into a room; there are too many parties helping to build solutions and they come and go as their help is needed and as their interest in working on the solution waxes and wanes. While braids are still imperfect in their capability to bring the right parties together at the right moment, the potential for superior performance in braids is much greater than a few people who lack the necessary knowledge sitting around a conference table and making stuff up.

Decision making. Traditional organizations have an advantage over braids in being able to make quick decisions. Braids have an advantage over traditional organizations in making the right decisions. At Red Hat, the difference between traditional decision making and decision making in the braid are striking,

> The primary responsibility for leaders at Red Hat is to build and support our meritocracy by making sure the right people are working together on the right things. The people who are closest to the issue, rather than those responsible for the overall direction of the organization or team, tend to make the decisions. This requires collaboration and mutual respect between associates and their managers, in a complementary relationship.

Traditional organizations make decisions on the best information available at the time. Leaders in traditional organizations pride themselves on their decision-making prowess. While they rely on their intuition to make calls when the facts are ambiguous, their preference is to have as much information as possible before they decide.

Braids also rely on information and intuition to make decisions although the information is of a different kind. Rather than gathering data about factors that could affect the decision, information is gained from trying things out, using iterative, design-thinking strategies. Braids don't have formal decision makers; they must respect the combined wisdom of the members of the braid. Doing this requires that parties who are in a position to act do so, on an experimental basis, so that more insights can be gained and fed back into the collective decision-making process. This approach produces a "step forward and a step back" path of progress, which may not inspire faith in the braid by traditional decision makers. However, the braid is more likely to learn from experience and adopt new solutions than traditional organizations, which tend to stick with poor decisions even in the face of evidence that those decisions are wrong.

Disruption. Finally, traditional organizations resist disruption, whereas braids are built to disrupt. If braids do not offer improved ways of doing things, there is really no reason for them to exist. In traditional organizations, the ties to positions, power, rewards, and other privileges of bureaucracies lock people in place. In braids, there are no such ties interfering with trying out different ways of doing things and the spirit of the braid is all about putting something new and better in place.

NOW GO DO IT

For all leaders, the message is, "It's time to get going." Braids are already here and are expected to grow in both number and importance to organizations of all kinds in the years to come. Life is full of change; for leaders, the move into a braided world is an important one.

The way to implement a braid is to begin by taking the first step. Implementing braids can seem like work and at times it almost certainly will involve long hours and a lot of effort. But as work goes, braids are interesting in that they both collaboration and learning. Braids will enable the accomplishment of things that would otherwise not be possible. That makes them a worthwhile investment.

EPILOGUE

MOVING ON

Towards Bioinspired and Evolving Organizations

Michel Zarka

Braided organizations are emerging to reinforce an important metamorphosis of organizations. From vertical, command-and-control, self-centered entities, companies are becoming more open, flexible, evolving and self-adaptative structures; driven more by human behavior and motivation rather than hierarchical rules and mechanistic processes. *Does this mean that rules, processes and hierarchies are disappearing?* In our view the answer is "no." No, because to a large degree these mechanistic elements will be fully digitalized (through data lakes for example), allowing for more agility and faster adaptability.

Figure 1 shows this metamorphosis of organizations:

The above metamorphosis will require five major shifts; most of which, currently, are nondominant elements in ways of working and the cultural mindset of Western organizations.

The Braided Organization:
Organization Design for a Digitally Connected World, pp. 133–137

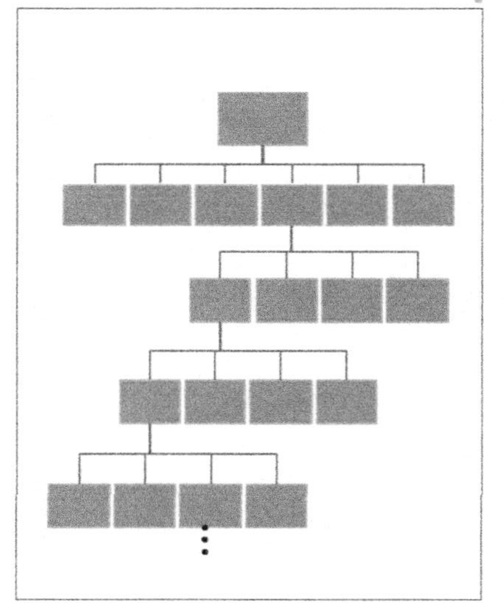

Vertical, fully ruled, self-centered organization

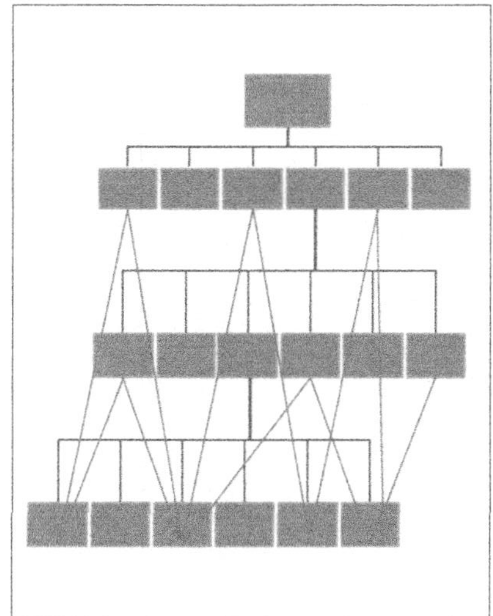

Internally braided organization with newly emergent collaborative patterns

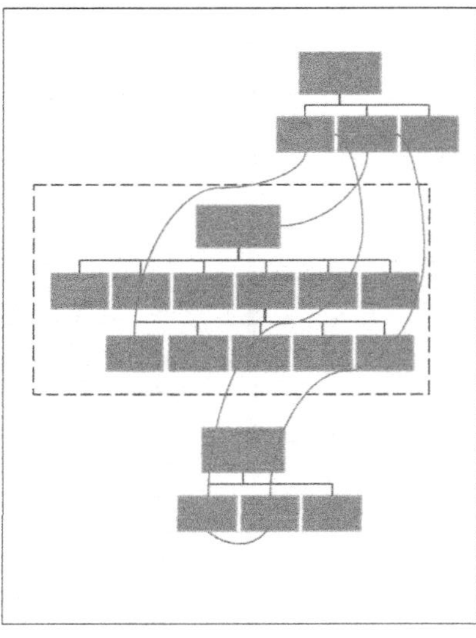

Openly braided organization, where collaboration extends beyond the boundary of the initial organization

Figure 1.

Mindshift #1 Hybridization: Value creation will move from ownership of exclusive know-how to hybridization of technologies, operating models and cultures

New hybridization patterns will emerge from a permanent convergence of bio/nano data with cognitive technologies across multiple industries. In the past, this convergence was limited to voice, data, and image which resulted in a merge of industries that were formerly independent. More hybridization will spring from new connections between diverse cultures of global and local enterprises as these entities operate more and more through the Internet, deal with international competition and customers, and tap into the extensive global data lakes of knowledge and insights. Greater blending across industries and cultures will occur from the invention of business models designed to challenge the existing highly segmented and specialized value chains. We already are seeing signs of this as the major players such as Amazon, Alibaba, cross the boundaries of their traditional business undertaking ventures in new sectors and industries.

Mindshift #2 Local and Multiscale Equilibrium: New end-to-end operating models will deliver simultaneously more customer focus and cost savings

Agility will be enhanced by the emergence of bioinspired ways of working and self-adapting systems rather than mechanistic approaches. The classical, functional, and sequential views of the organization, dominated by control and evaluation, will be progressively replaced by braiding around purposes or communities regardless of hierarchy or enterprise boundaries. The new self-controlling system will allow for more local trade-offs in the context of shared targets that will transform how results are evaluated and contributors are rewarded.

Mindshift #3 Sharing: Innovation will be enabled by more sharing of knowledge and assets rather than exclusive ownership

Bright ideas owned by individuals will continue to exist, nevertheless, the lack of open access to such "owned" ideas will drastically reduce their impact and thus lifetime. Therefore, the value of a new idea will be linked to its open access, availability, "sharability" as well as its speed of diffusion. In parallel, the innovativeness of a new product, idea or a concept will be more frequently challenged by the public and the digital "wise men," the power of the "experts in a domain" with the power of the anonymous nonexperts.

Mindshift #4 Pollination Leadership: The emergence of a new type of leader focused on cross-pollination of ideas—pollination leader—will strengthen interconnections and sustainability.

A new type of leadership will emerge replacing the known models of the hierarchical or influential leadership. A pollination leader, as we call it, is a leader capable of listening and understanding the ideas coming from within or outside the organization. Such a leader will have as an imperative to connect people and ideas to others with relevant insights, irrespective of their function or position in the organizational hierarchy. The objective for such a leader will be to build upon the established connections engaging the organization in "pollination" of ideas, projects, and insights.

Mindshift #5 Digitalization & Distributed Ownership of Purposes: Efficiency will be the outcome of a continued digitalization and distribution of ownership

By "efficiency" we refer to a number of elements: cost-effectiveness, quality of delivery, wellness in the workplace, team spirits, time to resolution, reduction of cycles, and openness to initiatives. For these efficiency outcomes, digitalization will play a major role in several ways: digitalization of knowledge will allow faster collaboration and problem-solving, real-time sharing of initiatives and responsibilities across the organization regardless of one's hierarchical position. Distributed ownership of purposes will allow individuals and braids to take responsibility for a common purpose and create an open environment enabling both an individual and collective responsibility while avoiding the siloed approach.

Start Experimenting With the New Mindsets

The mindset shifts described above could not be mandated by the top and thus cascaded down the organization. Doing so would imply a negation of braids and lead to the classical vertical, self-centered ways of operating. Therefore, such mind-shifts could only be the results of deliberate risk-taking through designed experiments with braids aiming at demonstrating the new value from open braiding and new ways of working.

We would encourage the readers of this book to take a leap of faith and start exploring the mind-shift associated with braided organizations by experimenting with one of the following

Hybridization: Co-innovation with X (customers, suppliers, others)

Local and multiscale equilibrium: Community based problem solving

Sharing: Digitalize your knowledge, experience
Pollination leadership: Identify leaders ready for a pollination challenge
Digitalization and distributed ownership of purposes: Digitalize key purposes

The more you engage in these experiences, the faster your progress will be to building a braided organization and reaping the benefits with which it is associated.

REFERENCES

Amin, A., Bargach, S., Donegan, J., Martin, C. Smith, R., Burgoyne, M., Censi, P., Day, P., & Kornberg, R. (2001). Building a knowledge-sharing culture. *Oilfield Review, Spring*, 45–68.

Arena, M. (2018). *Adaptive space: How GM and other companies are positively disrupting themselves and transforming into agile organizations.* New York, NY: McGraw Hill.

Bazigos,M., Gagnon, C., & Schaninger, B. (2016, January) Leadership in context. *McKinsey Quarterly*. Retrieved from https://www.mckinsey.com/business-functions/organization/our-insights/leadership-in-context

Bernstein, E., Bunch, J., Canner, N., & Lee, M. (2016). Beyond the holacracy hype. *Harvard Business Review*, *94*(7), 8.

Boarschberg, A. (2017). Personal conversation with author.

Brown, T. (2009). *Change by design: How design thinking creates new alternatives for business and society*. New York, NY: HarpersCollins Business.

Brynjolfsson, E., Rock, D., & Syverson, C. (2018). Artificial intelligence and the modern productivity paradox: A clash of expectations and statistics. In A. K. Agrawal, J. Gans, & A. Goldfarb (Eds.), *The economics of artificial intelligence: An agenda.* Chicago, IL: University of Chicago Press.

Corsi, P., & Michel, C. (2015, January). The way of the Solar Impulse Project. SIG Design Society. 8th SIG Design Theory Paris Workshop, 26th–27th.

Cross, R., Gray, P., Cunningham, S., Showers, M., & Thomas, R. (2010). How to make employee networks that really work. *Sloan Management Review,*

Bushe, G. R., & Shani, A. B. (1991). *Parallel learning structures*. Reading, MA, Addison-Welsey.

Chesbrough, H., Vanhaverbeke, W., & West, J. (2006). *Open innovation: Researching a new paradigm.* Oxford, England: Oxford University Press.

Christensen, C. (1997). *The innovator's dilemma.* Cambridge, MA: Harvard Business School Press.

Davenport, T. (1993). *Process innovation: Reengineering work through information technology*. Boston, MA: Harvard Business Press.

Drucker, P. (2014). *Innovation and entrepreneurship.* New York, NY: Routledge.

Dubois, P. (1979). *Sabotage in industry*. London, England: Penguin Books.

Gattorna, J. (2015). *Dynamic supply chains: How to design, build and manage people-centric value networks.* Harlow, UK: Pearson.

Grant, R. (2013). The development of knowledge management in the oil & gas industry. *Universia Business Review.* Retrieved from https://ubr.universia.net/article/viewFile/895/1021

Hackett, R. (2018, June). How JP Morgan Chase learned to love the blockchain. *Fortune*, 161–166.

Hackman, R., & Oldham, G. (1980). *Work redesign*. Reading, MA: Addison-Wesley.

Hammer, M., & Champy, J. (1993). *Reengineering the Corporation.* New York, NY: HarperCollins Business.

Huston, L., & Sakkab, N. (2006, March). Connect and develop. *Harvard Business Review*, *84*(3), 58–66.

Institute for Corporate Productivity. (2017). *Purposeful collaboration: The essential components of collaborative cultures*. Retrieved from www.i4cp.com

Kahneman, D. (2011). *Thinking, fast and slow*. New York, NY: Farrar, Straus and Giroux.

Kerr, S. (1975). On the folly of rewarding A, while hoping for B. *Academy of Management Journal*, *18*(4), 769–783.

Johansen, B. (2017). *The new leadership literacies: Thriving in a future of extreme disruption and distributed everything*. Oakland, CA: Berrett-Kohler.

Kotter, J. P. (2014). *Accelerate: Building strategic agility for a faster-moving world*. New York, NY: Harvard Business Review Press.

Lawler, E. E., & Worley, C. G. (2006). *Built to change: How to achieve sustained organizational effectiveness*. San Francisco, CA: Jossey Bass.

Leonardi, P., & Neeley, T. (2017, Nov–Dec). What managers need to know about social tools. *Harvard Business Review,* 118–126.

Lohr, S. (2016). G.E., the 124-year-old software start-up. In *The New York Times.* Retrieved from https://www.nytimes.com/2016/08/28/technology/ge-the-124-year-old-software-start-up.html

Manz, C., Shipper, F., & Stewart, G. (2009). Shared influence at WL gore & associates. *Organizational Dynamics*, *38*(3), 239–244.

McChrystal, S., Collins, T., Silverman, D., & Fussell, C. (2015). *Team of teams: new rules of engagement for a complex world.* London, England: Penguin Books.

McGonigal, J. (2011). *Reality is broken: Why games make us better and how they can change the world*. London, England: Penguin Books.

McGregor, D. (1960). *The human side of enterprise*. New York, NY: McGraw-Hill.

McGuire, J. B., & Rhodes, G. (2009). *Transforming your leadership culture*. San Francisco, CA: Jossey-Bass.

Nietzche, F. (1996). *All too human: A book for free spirits.* Cambridge, England: Cambridge University Press.

Oilfield Review. (2016, January). Schlumberger. Retrieved from chrome-extension://oemmndcbldboiebfnladdacbdfmadadm/https://www.slb.com/~/media/Files/resources/oilfield_review/ors16/Jan2016/Jan2016_Oilfield_Review.pdf

Page, T., Rahnema, A., Murphy, T., & McDowell, T. (2016). *Unlocking the flexible organization: Organizational design for an uncertain future*. USA: Deloitte Development.

Pasmore, W. (2015). *Leading continuous change*. Oakland, CA: Berrett-Koehler.

Patterson, K., Grenny, J. M., McMillan, R. R., & Switzler, A. (2002). *Crucial conversations: Tools for talking when stakes are high*. New York, NY: McGraw-Hill.

Pava, C. (1983). *Managing new office technology: an organizational strategy*. New York, NY: Free Press.

Pentland, A. (2015). *Social physics: How social networks can make us smarter*. London, England: Penguin Books.

Piccard (2016). Speech to the UN from the cockpit. Retrieved from https://www.youtube.com/watch?v=r1EVfr0diZY

Pfeffer, J., & Salancik, G. R. (1978). *The external control of organizations*. New York, NY: Harper and Row.

Purser, R., Pasmore, W., & Tenkasi, R. (1992). The influence of deliberations on learning in new product development teams. *Journal of Engineering and Technology Management, 9*, 1–28.

Solis, B. (2014). Digital Darwinism: How disruptive technology is changing business for good. *Wired*. Retrieved from https://www.wired.com/insights/2014/04/digital-darwinism-disruptive-technology-changing-business-good/

Schein, E. (1985). *Organizational culture and leadership*. San Francisco, CA: Jossey Bass.

Smith, C. A., Organ, D. W., & Near, J. P. (1983). Organizational citizenship behavior: Its nature and antecedents. *Journal of Applied Psychology, 68*(4), 653.

Surowiecki, J. (2005). *The wisdom of crowds*. New York, NY: Anchor Books.

Tushman, M. L., & O'Reilly, C. A. (2002). *Winning through innovations*. Boston, MA: Harvard Business School Publishing Corporation.

U.S. Census Bureau. (2017). Startup firms created over 2 million jobs in 2015. Retrieved from https://www.census.gov/newsroom/press-releases/2017/business-dynamics.html

Verne, J. (1875). *Twenty thousand leagues under the seas, or The Marvellous and Exciting Adventures of Pierre Aronnax, Conseil His Servant, and Ned Land, a Canadian Harpooner: Translated from the French*. New York, NY: Worthington.

Whitehurst, J. (2015). *The open organization: Igniting passion and performance*. Boston, MA: Harvard Business Press.

Wilson, J.. & Daugherty, P. (2018, July–August,). Humans and AI are joining forces. *Harvard Business Review*, 115–123.

Worley, C. G., Williams, T. D., Williams, T., & Lawler E. E., III. (2014). *The agility factor: Building adaptable organizations for superior performance*. Hoboken, NJ: John Wiley & Sons.

Zand, D. E. (1974). Collateral organization: A new change strategy. *The Journal of Applied Behavioral Science, 10*(1), 63–89.

ABOUT THE AUTHORS

Michel Zarka and Founder of Theano Advisors, a global management consulting firm. Michel specializes in large-scale organizational transformation, including the complex transformation of sociotechnical systems. He has worked with international corporations in the U.S., U.K., France, Italy, and Germany. He holds a PhD degree in Mathematics with specialization in Game Theory and has written several books, including a book entitled *Repenser l'entreprise - Saisir ce qui commence, vingt regards sur une idée neuve,* published in 2007.

Elena Kochanovskaya is an Advisor to CEOs and Executives on organizational transformation and leadership effectiveness topics, including CEO impact and executive team development. She advises newly appointed CEOs and leaders in charge of implementing disruptive change agendas and new strategies. Elena has worked with CEOs and senior leaders from Fortune 500 companies in the U.S., U.K., France, Germany, Canada, and Bermuda. She is a graduate of McGill University and holds a MA degree in Industrial/Organizational Psychology from New York University.

William Pasmore is Senior Vice President at The Center for Creative Leadership and Professor of Practice at Teachers College, Columbia University. He is the author and editor of numerous books and articles, including his 2015 book, *Leading Continuous Change.* He is a true scholar practitioner, consulting to CEOs around the globe on matters pertaining to leadership and strategic change. Bill holds a PhD in Administrative Sciences from Purdue University.

Printed in Great Britain
by Amazon